PLAYSCRIPT 94

THE HANG OF THE GAOL
Heaven

Howard Barker

JOHN CALDER · LONDON
RIVERRUN PRESS · NEW YORK

First published in Great Britain, 1982, by
John Calder (Publishers) Ltd.,
18 Brewer Street, London W1R 4AS

All performing rights in these plays are strictly reserved and
applications for performance should be made to:
Judy Daish Associates Ltd.,
122 Wigmore Street,
London W1H 9FE

No performance of these plays may be given unless a licence has been obtained
prior to rehearsal.

British Library Cataloguing in Publication Data
Barker, Howard
  The hang of the gaol; and, Heaven.
  — (Playscript; 94)
  I. Title   II. Barker, Howard. Heaven III. Series
  822'.914   PR6052.A6485
ISBN 0 7145 3769 1 Paperback only

Typeset in 9/10 point Times by Ged Lennox Design, Cheltenham.
Printed by The Hillman Press, Frome.

CONTENTS

By the same author

Stage Plays

Cheek
No One Was Saved
Alpha Alpha
Edward, The Final Days
Stripwell
Claw
Fair Slaughter
The Love of a Good Man
That Good Between Us
The Hang of the Gaol
The Loud Boy's Life
No End of Blame
The Poor Man's Friend

TV Plays

Cows
Mutinies
Prowling Offensive
Conrod
Heroes of Labour
Russia
All Bleeding
Heaven

Radio Plays

One Afternoon on the 63rd Level of the North Face of the Pyramid of Cheops The Great
Henry V in Two Parts
Herman with Millie and Mick

THE HANG OF THE GAOL

The Hang of the Gaol *was first performed at the RSC's Warehouse Theatre in Covent Garden on 15th December 1978 with the following cast:*

COOPER	Edward Jewesbury
JANE	Lynn Farleigh
UDY	Colin McCormack
WHIP	Charles Wegner
BLOON	Iain Mitchell
DOCKERILL	Jeffery Kissoon
STAGG	Christopher Benjamin
TURK	Nigel Terry
JARDINE	Fulton Mackay
MATHESON	Gaye Brown
PONTING	Nicholas Le Prevost
ANGELA	Michele Copsey
Directed by	William Alexander

ACT ONE

Scene One

The burned out shell of Middenhurst Gaol, England. The GOVERNOR, *standing in the debris, looks around. His wife is standing nearby.*

COOPER.   A bucket-shitter did this. In some kidney of the wing. In some pissy, toxic corner of the night. Plotted it. Just look.

JANE..   Taxpayer's ulcer bursts. John Betjeman prostrate with shock.

COOPER.   My lovely ringing corridors of English iron. Struck sparks off the heels of warders' boots.

JANE.   Probably what started it.

COOPER.   My girders bearing in their grace the criminals' sleep . . .

JANE.   Glass and concrete next time. Abstract carpet in the Recreation Room. Choice of seven breakfasts, etcetera.

COOPER.   Some wept. Did I tell you that some wept? Shaken from their fetid blankets, in the alarm bells and the lights of army trucks, the tears came oozing. You would have thought it was their mother's house. So much history, one said, the flames flickering in his swimming blinkers. And this practically a tenant of Punishment Block before I came. The human condition. Magic thing. *(He walks further, gazing.)*

JANE.   We lose our gardeners, I suppose?

COOPER.   Yes. Jane must weed herself. Must get dirt on her own knees for once.

JANE *(shrugs)*.   Let it ramble.

COOPER.   Alternatively, yes.

JANE.   And who will take the dogs out? *(He looks sternly at her. Pause.)*

COOPER.   I am in the ashes of a lifetime.

JANE.   Sorry. Was wondering, that's all.

COOPER.   In another context, please. Considerations of that sort.

JANE.   Yes. Sorry. Yes. *(He walks away from her staring at the sky.)*

COOPER *(turning to her)*.   Mustn't hate them. The bucket-shitters. Once you hate them, chuck it up. Though they burn my crystal palace, I will bear no ill.

WHIP *and* UDY *come in, blue macs over their uniforms.*

UDY.   Good-morning, Colonel and Mrs Cooper.

COOPER.   Not good, Mr Udy. In all honesty. We have no prison any more.

UDY. The wiring was of Roman origin. I submitted Christ knows how many memoranda on the subject of the Roman wiring. Unfortunately, no higher authority thought fit to heed. *(He looks up.)* Oh, look, the sky!

COOPER. This was no short-circuit, Mr Udy. Unless it was in someone's brain . . .

UDY *(still gazing up).* Swallows! Who'd have thought C Block was under a migration trail?

COOPER. However repulsive the prospect, we shall have to drink at our own puddle first.

UDY *(looking at him).* Sorry?

COOPER. This fire blazed on the liquor of our sins. *(Pause.* WHIP *and* UDY *stare at him.)*

JANE. Colonel Cooper is desperately tired. Having been up all night. Smoke in his eyes and so on. *(To* COOPER*)* Shall we shove? *(Pause.)*

COOPER. They don't believe me. They will persist it is the wiring. They will have it a stray spark did all this. The Corporal's intellect.

He turns, drifts away, followed by JANE, *who stops, and looks back.*

JANE. About the borzois. They have daily doings, and my bucket-shitter's gone to Parkhurst with the rest.

UDY. I will find you an exerciser, Mrs Cooper. An officer, if I can't rake up anybody else. And if no officer, I will take them peeing myself.

JANE. Ta.

She goes out. UDY *and* WHIP *watch them disappear.*

WHIP. Roy. Will you find my head and screw it back on?

UDY. Quite.

WHIP. **Jesus!**

UDY. Don't be flabbergasted, Michael. I hate people being flabbergasted. It's a compliment.

WHIP *(persisting).* The liquor of our **what**?

UDY *(moving away from him).* I heard him, thank you very much.

Pause. WHIP *looks at* UDY *anxiously.*

WHIP. Roy.

UDY. What?

WHIP. This means an inquiry.

UDY *(gazing up nonchalantly).* What, another one?

WHIP. We have lost the prison.

UDY. So we have. *(Pause.)*

WHIP. Inquiries, Roy.

UDY. All right.

WHIP. Don't like 'em.

UDY. No one does.

WHIP. Me specially.

UDY. Your famous shyness.

WHIP. I go all —

UDY. Silly.

WHIP. Yes, I do.

UDY. Blush 'n' Stutter.

WHIP. Can't help it.

UDY. No indeed. *(Pause, then he looks down from the sky at last.)* In the beginning, England was a bear garden. It was a paradise for yobbos, Michael. Infinitely more so than it is now, hard as that may be to contemplate. There was no neighbourliness. Probably, had someone been able to conceive of neighbourliness, he would have had his brains splattered around the jungle with a club. They were that wild, our forbears. Though I have sometimes glimpsed that wildness in the yellow of a convict's eye, by and large it is eradicated, bred out like long-legged dachshunds or hair on a woman's arse. Are you listening?

WHIP. I love your stories, Roy.

UDY. It came to pass, in this unspecific time I am referring to, that a majority of English yobbos, weary of endless slash and chivvy, agreed to offer up their rights to one sole ruler, who would adjudicate and carry out the GBH on their behalf. When this happened, we don't know. In the darkest crevice of the past. But it happened, and we got THE LAW. It was a charming moment in the story of the world. It has been compared to the Garden of Eden.

WHIP. Who by?

UDY. By me, for one. All right?

WHIP. Okay.

UDY. But it was destined not to last. Astonishing to contemplate, the yobbo who had been entrusted with the precious instrument showed inclinations to unscrupulosity.

WHIP. Unwhat?

UDY *(pausing, looking darkly at him)*. Michael, do not resist the little education you are offered in this life. It will help you when you blush in front of bureaucrats.

WHIP.   I queried the word. Sorry.

UDY.   Never mind the words. Heed the message. *(Pause.)*

WHIP.   Go on.

UDY.   The law, this treasure of the human spirit, was seen to admit of much abuse. Stirrings in the masses threatened the return of yobbo culture. Jungle manners were on the cards again. Then someone thought of THE INQUIRY. *(Pause.)*

WHIP.   Ah. *(Pause. UDY lets it sink in.)*

UDY.   Whoever this philanthropic individual was is shrouded in the mists of centuries. All we know is that he bore the English way of life upon his shoulders and carried it safe through the sucking mud of discontent. His unsculptured statue lurks over every door of government. His comic genius gives shine to the cap badge of every cop and screw. For THE INQUIRY, Michael, protects you. Never was so much distance placed between a grievance and its object. Wrath dies from lack of nourishment, and revenge is withered by delay. Learn to love inquiries, Michael, for they love you. No one ever died from injuries received from two hundred pages of H.M. stationery.

Pause. WHIP *looks at him.*

WHIP.   Brilliant. As per usual.

UDY.   The power of vocabulary.

WHIP.   I never knew a screw like it.

UDY *(wandering along the hall)*.   Funny, when the language in a gaol is so pitifully thin. There are less than twenty words in the average con's vocabulary, and nearly all of them related to the functions.

WHIP.   A pity more didn't show up to your language class.

UDY.   What use is language to them? Words are an encumbrance. A merchant needs words, but a thief has eyes. A seducer needs his language, but a rapist gets there with a knife . . .

WHIP *(gazing at the ruins)*.   I am gonna miss it, Roy . . .

UDY.   Yes, we all are.

WHIP.   Dear ol' gaol . . . *(Pause.)*

UDY.   Are you gonna shit in it?

WHIP.   What?

UDY.   You heard.

WHIP.   Shit in it?

UDY.   The old screws never left a gaol without depositing a turd in it.

WHIP.   Burglar's trick.

UDY.   Superstition, obviously. One I adhere to. Sort of symbolic clearing out. Shedding of guilt. *(He looks round quickly.)* Anybody coming?

WHIP.   I don't think I will.

UDY *(removing his coat and jacket)*.   Help you, Michael. Face the inquiry with an open mind. My old man left turds in Dartmoor, Parkhurst, Reading, Pentonville. Never put a foot wrong. Died in bed.

WHIP.   Can't hurt, I s'pose. No one's gonna have to clear it up.

UDY.   Only a bulldozer, and that isn't going to take offence.

UDY *has his trousers down and crouches.* WHIP *quickly undresses.*

UDY.   They had an arrangement, the old screws did. The departing screw would say, I'm dropping in C Hall tonight. Then one of the other scews would shovel it up for him. Then when he left, someone would do the same for him. **Christ, who's that!**

WHIP *(jerking his trousers on again)*.   Somebody's coming!

UDY.   Sod it.

WHIP *(dragging on his braces)*.   I didn't manage it.

UDY.   Bad luck.

WHIP *(nervously)*.   Is it?

UDY *(dressing calmly)*.   What?

WHIP.   Bad luck?

UDY *(putting his jacket on)*.   Could be. Always another chance.

WHIP.   Come back tonight.

UDY.   Why don't you?

WHIP.   I will. Don't worry.

Two young men in white coats come in.

UDY.   Good morning, gentlemen. Can we help you?

BLOON/DOCKERILL.   We are the Fire Inspectorate.

UDY.   Well, you've come to the right place, haven't you?

BLOON *(gazing disapprovingly about)*.   They put a lot of water into it.

WHIP.   It puts the flames out, doesn't it?

DOCKERILL.   Yes, but we prefer to work with dry material, don't we?

BLOON.   Gone over the top again.

DOCKERILL.   Drowned it.

BLOON.   You can't tell firemen, can you?

DOCKERILL.   You say 'Please don't saturate it because we are hunters after clues, and nothing is more inimical to clues than thirty-thousand gallons of cold water.' You arrive and what do you find?

BLOON.   Thirty-thousand gallons of cold water.

DOCKERILL.   You get fucked off with it, sometimes.

UDY.   I'll make life easy for you. Unofficially, of course. It was the wiring. *(Pause. The inspectors look at* UDY.*)*

BLOON.   Here we go again.

DOCKERILL.   Olé.

UDY.   Sorry?

BLOON.   Have we ever?

DOCKERILL.   Never. But **never.**

UDY.   Never what?

BLOON.   Been to a job without somebody saying —

BLOON/DOCKERILL.   **It's the wiring!** *(They burst out laughing.* UDY *stares.)*

UDY.   Sorry I spoke. *(He looks to* WHIP.*)* Remind me not to offer bona fide advice.

WHIP.   I think we're in the way, Roy. *(He starts to go out.)*

UDY *(to the inspectors).*   Don't hesitate to ask if you need anything. I'll burst out laughing.

WHIP *and* UDY *go out. Unabashed, the inspectors click open their brief-cases.*

DOCKERILL.   Usual superb facilities.

BLOON.   Coffee boiling.

DOCKERILL.   Sandwiches.

BLOON/DOCKERILL.   **Oh, sorry, everything's in such a mess!** *(Pause, while they unpack various items.)*

BLOON.   Forgot the acetate.

DOCKERILL.   Naughty.

BLOON.   I'll forget my head one day.

DOCKERILL.   Quote.

BLOON.   Thank you.

DOCKERILL *(holding some bottles).*   No table.

BLOON.   Surprise, surprise.

DOCKERILL.   Or lunch, I take it.

BLOON/DOCKERILL *(instantly).*   **What do you expect, a three-course dinner? There's been a fire here, darling!** *(They lay out their equipment on the floor.)*

DOCKERILL.   That's my pencil.

BLOON.   What is?

DOCKERILL.   In your lily-white hand.

BLOON.   Oh, yes. It's got your name on.

DOCKERILL.   Be my guest.

BLOON.   You don't mean it!

DOCKERILL.   I **want** you to have it.

BLOON.   Darling!

BLOON/DOCKERILL.   **Give it 'ere you fucking cunt!**

BLOON *throws the pencil over to* DOCKERILL, *then proceeds to unwind a tape-measure, walking to the back wall.* DOCKERILL *whistles as he works on a note book. Pause.*

BLOON.   Ivor Novello.

DOCKERILL.   Warmish.

WHIP.   Kern.

DOCKERILL *(shaking a bottle)*.   Struggling. Struggling.

BLOON.   Another bar. *(DOCKERILL whistles a single note.)* Gershwin!

DOCKERILL *(triumphantly)*.   Two hundred and fifty-six!

BLOON *(Pretending to shoot himself)*.   Aaaaaaggghhh!

DOCKERILL *(walking to a wall with his bottle)*.   Two hundred and fifty-six.

BLOON.   What? What?

DOCKERILL.   A most convincing four point lead—

BLOON/DOCKERILL.   **Shall we make it twenty p. a point?**

BLOON.   Come on, what is it?

DOCKERILL.   Moonlight. Sammy Jacobs.

He starts scraping the wall and collecting the dust in a plastic bag.

BLOON.   I love you, too.

DOCKERILL.   Oh, do you, heart?

BLOON *(stepping back as he winds the tape in)*.   **Someone's had a shit in here!**

As he pulls a face of disgust. STAGG *enters, his overcoat open, a cigarette in his mouth. He gazes at the ruined roof.*

STAGG.   I don't blame 'em. I am a bit of a rebel myself. If you stuck me in a room ten foot by twelve I might have a go at burning it. I might make a bonfire of the sheets. *(He turns to the inspectors.)* Good morning, lads. William Stagg. Home Secretary. *(They nod distantly at him.)* Ignore me. I am what our friends in the papers call a ghoul. No one knows I'm here yet. It was malicious, I suppose?

DOCKERILL.   Sorry?

STAGG.   The blaze. The conflagration, son.

DOCKERILL.   Only just got here ourselves.

STAGG.   Hot foot, eh? Get it? Hot foot? *(He points to the floor.)* Funny how they keep the heat. I was in Glasgow when eight kids were burned. I was round there like a shot. Took me round the back, to look. Eight little black things in tarpaulin. I could have wept. I never knew a brick could burn. What is it about the Scots, I wonder? Paraffin? *(He moves across and stands behind* DOCKERILL, *who is scraping the wall. Pause.)* I said before I left home this morning, to my wife this was, to Audrey, can you put a figure on the damage down at Middenhurst? Get it right within two noughts and I'll buy you a rabbit fur. Rabbit, she wants. We're both against seal-hunting and fox-hunting and all the posh barbarity that passes for sport in this democratic land of ours. So she writes a number on the Kelloggs box. 300 million. I wouldn't be surprised she's right, on this week's figures. By the time the contractors have scuttled though, the Bovises, MacAlpines and that mob, 3,000 million might be more appropriate. Did it start in here?

BLOON.   Yes.

STAGG.   What he must have gone through.

BLOON.   Who?

STAGG.   The arsonist. What he must have suffered. . . . Or was it just a gesture that got out of hand? There are nine hundred cell fires in HM Prisons every year. Gestures, all of them. Then one goes further, and three-hundred-million comes tumbling out the public purse. That's two hospitals. Or a pair of submarines. I bet he never thought of that . . . *(He walks a little way, stops.)* Well, I haven't been discovered yet. How does a man get a cup of tea round here?

BLOON.   Says he's Home Secretary, I suppose.

STAGG.   Well, I'm not averse to pulling rank. Socialists have got to drink like everybody else. *(He goes off left and shouts)* Hello! Hello? Tell someone Mr Stagg is here and dry as the floorboards at party conference! Never mind. Just bring some tea. *(He reappears. Pause. They work on.)* I wonder if I might ask you something. You as two ordinary working gents. White collar British workers. How do I come across? *(Pause. They do not respond.)* Thought that might shock you. I ask because I have an image which in some ways I resent. An image dreamed up by the proprietors of newspapers, individuals not widely celebrated for their dedication to the truth, or the good of England come to that. In this image I am on the rude side. I drop clangers. How much of that is witch-hunting, and how much truth? *(Pause.)* Silence reigned and we all got wet. *(Pause.)* Come on, I call myself a democrat. *(Pause.)*

DOCKERILL.   Yes.

STAGG.   What?

DOCKERILL.   You are a big-mouthed cunt. *(Silence.)*

STAGG.   Fair enough. You are in the Nazi party, I suppose.

DOCKERILL.   No.

STAGG.   I ask because of your preference for abuse. *(DOCKERILL shrugs.)* I ask because while you sport a technician's neutral overcoat you are a thug. *(He shrugs again.)* I could cheerfully land you one on the chin.

DOCKERILL.   Doubtless.

STAGG.   Because I can box.

DOCKERILL.   Okay.

STAGG.   And you took advantage of me. Do you box?

DOCKERILL.   No.

STAGG.   Naturally. You wouldn't, would you?

DOCKERILL.   Never.

STAGG.   In any case, I am a member of the Cabinet. So you are pretty safe aren't you?

DOCKERILL.   Look, you asked me —

STAGG.   **Aren't you! Perfectly safe?** *(Pause.)*

DOCKERILL.   Yes.

STAGG *(glaring at him).*   Christ. What a specimen. *(He shakes his head. JANE enters, with a tray containing tea and biscuits. She picks her way over the charred floor.)* Good Heavens, it's a lady.

JANE.   Welcome to Middenhust.

STAGG.   You tread like a mannequin through the ashes of obscure miseries, Madam. If you follow me.

JANE.   I was a mannequin. I am Jane Cooper, the Governor's wife. My husband is asleep for the first time in forty hours.

STAGG.   I wouldn't wake him for the world. I'm afraid I don't always arrive announced. Like Jesus, I appear with dusty feet. That way I find things out. Such as that people think I am a loud-mouthed whatsit. And I am also spared a police guard, which these days is certain death. In my Ford Granada I could be a travelling salesman, couldn't I, though the glass can stop a rocket. Will you join me? I shall be embarrassed sipping on my own. *(He goes to the teapot.)*

JANE.   There is only one cup.

STAGG.   So there is. Well, I better have it, then. Will you pour? I have heard it's unlucky if someone pours who didn't make the tea.

JANE.   I didn't make the tea.

STAGG.   Of course not. Silly me. Well, it makes no difference, then. *(He pours it carefully,* JANE *holding the tray. The inspectors watch. He puts the sugar in. He sips.)* And when would you have been a mannequin, Mrs Cooper?

JANE.   In the fifties. I modelled something called the Austerity Gown. It was made of fifteen yards of Chinese silk. I remember someone being hanged. And there were ration books.

STAGG.   It wasn't such a green and pleasant land was it?

JANE.   I preferred it.

STAGG.   Did you? I suppose these things depend on which side of privilege you stood. I was a plumber while you tottered up and down the ramp.

JANE.   And now you're Home Secretary.

STAGG.   Something had to give. It was that or bishops on the lamp-posts.

JANE.   My husband is a little bit upset.

STAGG.   Of course.

JANE.   I don't mean a little bit.

STAGG.   You mean a lot. Funny how the English will persist in understatement. A way to look unruffled, I expect. *(Pause.)* Whereas he is ruffled, is he? *(He puts the cup on the tray.)*

JANE.   Yes.

STAGG.   Well, it is one of our biggest prisons that's got lost. I don't think Colonel Cooper would be normal if he wasn't ruffled. I would be. Bloody ruffled.

JANE.   He blames himself.

STAGG.   Yes, that is the nature of responsibility, isn't it? I respect it, though it's going out of fashion. I think Colonel Cooper would do better to let an inquiry find who did it, if anybody did. In any case I don't see blame entering into it. Blame is medieval, isn't it?

JANE.   I don't think it's blame he's bothered about. I think it's guilt.

STAGG. Ah. Well, I'm a politician. It's t'other way about with us. Shall we be moving? It's draughty in here without a roof.

JANE *(leading off)*. It always was. But bucket-shitters aren't entitled to a lot of comfort, are they?

STAGG *(stopping in his tracks)*. Sorry? Come again?

JANE. They aren't entitled to a lot of —

STAGG. No. You called them —

JANE. Bucket-shitters. *(Pause. He stares.)* I thought everybody called them that.

STAGG. No.

JANE. Well, they do shit in buckets, don't they?

STAGG. Yes, but —

JANE. They don't have lavs?

STAGG. In some of the older institutions, unhappily.

JANE. Well, that's it, then, isn't it?

STAGG. Mrs Cooper, it's pejorative. *(She walks out. STAGG looks at the inspectors, shaking his head.)* The squirearchy. You cannot wipe the bleeders out. *(He follows her out. The inspectors go on working. Suddenly they turn to each other.)*

BLOON/DOCKERILL. **A'm a bit of a rebel myself!**

DOCKERILL. Audrey, Audrey, listen Aud —

BLOON *(falsetto)*. My rabbit, my rabbit —

DOCKERILL. Pass t'Kellogs, Aud —

BLOON *(falsetto)*. My bleeding rabbit —

DOCKERILL. Pass t'sugar, love —

BLOON *(falsetto)*. My fucking rabbit, you miserable shit!

BLOON/DOCKERILL. **I could cheerfully land you one on the chin!**

They continue working, shaking test tubes and holding them up to the light.

BLOON *(looking at the result)*. Snot electrical.

DOCKERILL. Definitely snot.

BLOON. Sdeliberate.

DOCKERILL. Smalicious.

BLOON/DOCKERILL. **S'time for a drink!**

They put down their instruments, wipe their hands on rags and reach for their jackets. BLOON combs his hair.

BLOON.　My conflagration begins in the basement laundry of a loony bin.

DOCKERILL.　Sick. Sick.

BLOON.　A loon, in a fit of imagined dehydration, has consumed one litre of chemical cleanser, say —

DOCKERILL.　Thawpit.

BLOON.　Say Thawpit. Anything with a chloride base.

DOCKERILL.　Sick. Sick.

BLOON.　Proceeds to roll himself a particularly loony cigarette.

DOCKERILL.　Malcolm, may I ask, why is it your fires have to involve spontaneous combustion?

BLOON.　And taking a Swan Vesta, gracefully, as befits an inoffensive loon, ignites the phosphorous —

DOCKERILL.　Goodbye, lunatic.

BLOON *(going out)*.　There is an explosion.

DOCKERILL *(adjusting his tie as he follows)*.　Unrecognizable pieces of flaming lunatic attach themselves to the surrounding walls and laundry baskets.

BLOON.　The sprinkler system —

BLOON/DOCKERILL.　**Has an unidentifiable fault!**

They go out, laughing. After some time, the sound of shufflling feet is heard. TURK enters, swaying on plimsolls and pushing a broom. He wears prison denims and carries a bucket. Dumping down the bucket, he begins swabbing the floor. After a while, a voice off.

UDY.　Turk, you silly fucker! What are you doing with that broom! *(TURK freezes. UDY appears, looks at him.)* Turk, you cannot sweep the venerable floor, old son. The floor hath no further need of it. *(TURK is a picture of confusion.)* You shouldn't be here, should you? You should be somewhere altogether different. Somewhere where they specialize in people's heads. How come you aren't on the Isle of Wight?

TURK.　Isle of Wight?

UDY.　Oh, Jesus.

TURK.　No one said nothing about the Isle of Wight.

UDY.　Everybody else is on the Isle of Wight.

TURK.　Why, Mr Udy?

UDY.　Are you being wilfully pig-ignorant? If so, I issue my first warning. Why aren't you on the Isle of Wight?

TURK.　I can't think, Mr Udy.

UDY. My second warning. Swift on its heels. Why aren't you on the Isle of Wight?

TURK. Christ. Erm. Erm. Christ.

UDY. I'm booking you. *(He takes out a notebook.)*

TURK. 7787. Turk. Joseph.

UDY. Well, Turk Joseph, as you're still here, the Governor's borzois need a shit.

TURK. I was on my way there, Mr Udy. *(He picks up his bucket.)*

UDY. Are there any more like you?

TURK. Are there any more like me?

UDY. I don't mean barmy, I mean definitely not on the Isle of Wight?

TURK. I haven't seen nobody else today.

UDY. Funny, ain't it?

TURK. Very strange.

UDY *(pointing to the sky)*. Look up there, Turk, and tell me what you see. *(*TURK *looks up. Pause.)* Will you? What do you see?

TURK. Birds, Mr Udy.

UDY. Ever seen birds there before?

TURK. Can't say I have.

UDY. In how many crawling years?

TURK. Six, Mr Udy.

UDY. Six years and never seen birds up there before.

TURK. Unusual.

UDY. Very. You are a liar and a hypocrite. Get out before I double book you. *(*TURK *starts going out.)* **Turk! Where did you spend the sodding night?**

TURK *(baffled)*. On Number 7 landing, sir. *(They look at one another.)* Why, did something happen? *(He shuffles out, watched by* UDY. *Pause.)*

UDY. When I was a young screw, when I was a fresh young turnkey and came in whistling through the gate, they took me to the armoury, they said upon the sounding of three hooters run here, let there be a clattering of your boots on cobbles and the echo of your shouts against the flags, for this is RIOT. And they showed how with a roar of chains the cutlasses were freed from their oily sockets, and the blue steel grinned at me, slimy with a little grease. Oh, Cutlass, our young straight eyes were fixed on you while Instructor Peachy, was it, Peach or something, said it is a slashing weapon, it has a downward stroke ideal for neutralizing men in corridors, it has a profile which clamps terror in the dry mouths of felons rioting. And never did I walk a landing or supervise their exercise but Cutlass was beside me. Cutlass was my best mate in his granite armoury, blue-greased and waiting for our yelling boots. Mr Udy, they say, of all the screws you know the littlest of fear. It's Cutlass, I say. Because of Cutlass I can be your friend, no matter how you're hissing.

Sound of borzois barking. Fade to black.

Scene Two

The moors. TURK *enters breathless, holding a pair of dogs' leads. He stares at the shell of the gaol in the distance, sways like a classic drunkard, points with an inebriated finger.*

TURK.   Hey. . . . Hey! *(He strains to look, head forward.)* No fockin' gaol. . . . **No fockin' gaol there's not!** *(He sways.)* A say . . . cum back this instant, will ya? Gaol. Cum back. *(He wags his finger at it.)* Listen . . . listen . . . no . . . listen. . . . **Listen will ya! Ya can't just booger off . . . not if yoo're a focking gaol ya can't.** . . . *(He staggers, almost falls.)* No . . . no . . . ya not listenin'. **A'm tellin' ya aren't a!** *(The borzois begin barking.)* Shuddup will ya! A'm talkin' to the focking **Gaol** aren't A . . . *(Silence.)* Thank yoo . . . thank yoo . . . very much *(He jabs his finger at the distance.)* Noo fockin' right   . . . *(Pause. He grins.)* Ain't never seen a fockin' dead gaol before. A take ma hat off . . . *(The dogs bark.)* **Shuddup will ya! Have ya noo fockin' respect?** *(They are silent.)* Show a bit a proper decency . . .

He mimes removing a hat, bowing very low, then stumbles drunkenly, giggling. As he sinks to the ground. COOPER *appears, in a dressing gown. He watches* TURK *for a few moments.* TURK, *aware of him, stands up smartly.*

TURK.   Good day for dogs, Mr Cooper. *(Pause.* COOPER *looks at him for some time.)*

COOPER.   I'm not to have sleep. I have been on the bed five hours. She won't come to me, the tart sleep. Anyone can have her except me, apparently. *(Pause.)*

TURK.   There's a hint of lameness in the rear right of the bitch.

COOPER.   You should have warned me, Turk. Why did you never warn me?

TURK.   I saw nothing, Colonel.

COOPER.   Where I was stepping wrong. Why they were rising up against me.

TURK.   I saw nothing.

COOPER.   Your curt little statement. Your trim little mouth.

TURK.   There it is.

COOPER.   I bleed from this. When we were out to build Heaven here, I bleed from this! *(TURK looks embarrassed.)* I need not tell you of the gaols where governors practise golf strokes to the sound of petitions being read, where architects deformed by corruption dine with them as their honoured guests. It was clean here. It was no grafting, sticky club. I ran it just.

TURK.   I could muzzle her if you want to look.

COOPER.   **Fuck the bitch!** The smoked granite of my prison is scratching at my eyeball.

TURK.   **All this desperation. You, who never sweated, who was a byword on the landings for the cleanliness of his linen. Now in a dressing-gown, jabbering with stubble on his chin.**

COOPER.   You may not tease me. Dressing-gown notwithstanding. Know your place.

TURK.   You have been disgoverned, Colonel Cooper. You are the lord of demolition now.

COOPER.   I hold the Queen's appointment.

TURK.   Piece of paper, Colonel. For all its embossing and discreet red edge.

COOPER.   She signed it. That is all you need to know. Let every bucket-shitter tremble beneath Elizabeth.

TURK.   Today, you sound illiberal. But as you say, smoke gets in your eyes. Tomorrow you will be your old solicitous self, I bet. You will be all welfare and self-criticism, apologies, and even tears.

COOPER.   Tears? You've seen my tears?

TURK.   I have done. But never told the others. They would mistake your very prominent humanity for weakness. They would call you woman and piss at your image in the showers.

COOPER.   You miss nothing, do you Turk? When I chose you as my peach I was very sound.

TURK.   I miss nothing, and I have reason to believe I may be sane. There are few you could attach that word to who have served six years in this place. *(He looks off, right.)* Your wife is coming. Either for you or the dogs. *(He walks a little, and, adopting an accent calls out.)* **Sheba! Leave bluddy rabbit, tha good lass!**

COOPER.   Stay close to me, Turk. Your hand in the nightmare I could do with. *(TURK looks at him, then moves away, rattling the chain.)*

TURK.   **Cum 'ere will thee! My leggy lass, chuck rabbit chasing, cum on, now!**

JANE *comes in, accompanied by* STAGG.

STAGG.   Colonel Cooper, I presume? I love your outfit. No doubt easier to wriggle out of in a bog.

JANE.   This is our Home Secretary, Stagg.

COOPER.   We have rancoured on the telephone.

STAGG.   So we have done. On the killers-on-parole issue. Reconciling progressive penology with public tolerance is the quickest way to the opposition benches I can think of. One ungrateful maniac can cost you an election, take my word for it.

COOPER.   I do.

STAGG.   Good. Because the nation must be governed and God help you if the other lot get in. It'll be doors locked at seven and no chess sets, take my word for it.

JANE *(to* TURK*)*.   Turk, you managed not to be despatched.

TURK *(dialect)*.   Missed bus, missus.

JANE *(imitating him)*.   Missed bus, he says.

STAGG.   Glad of this walk. Stuck in the car from Whitehall, bunched up innards, veins all cramped. Can't be good for you. I jog, but there's no comparison with this. There will have to be an inquiry, Cooper, but you'll have gathered that.

COOPER.   Why?

STAGG.   Good one. I am all for basic questions. I was addressing the coppers' graduation whatnot down at Hendon this time last week, and a kid said, this will grease his progress, won't it, do we really need a police force? Silence. Silence you could walk on. But it made me think. Like you say, why? I am all for asking why. Inquiries are a sort of reflex, aren't they? Something happens, bang, we have a load of geezers sipping gin and tonic while HM Government picks up the bill.

COOPER.   Why, then?

STAGG.   Well, rule of thumb on this one, isn't it? It's a matter of public concern. Christ, look at that dog!

TURK.   **Cum 'ere! Cum 'ere, Rhodesia, cum 'ere, boy!**

STAGG.   Rhodesia?

JANE.   Yes. It's a place in Africa.

STAGG.   Zimbabwe, surely?

JANE.   You are free to call it what you like.

STAGG.   I will do.

JANE.   Likewise me and my dog.

STAGG.   You're right, of course. Call it Hitler if you want.

COOPER.   I asked you why.

STAGG.   You asked and I told you. A prison goes up like a Roman candle and we don't know why. I couldn't dodge it if I wanted to. There are questions on the order paper now.

COOPER.   This is a matter for me and my officers.

STAGG.   Ah, the old cry.

COOPER.   It is our place.

STAGG.   It is, and great weight will be given to your evidence.

COOPER.   Evidence?

TURK.   **'Ey, 'ey, 'ey, Rhodesia, tha great stoopid animal!**

STAGG.   Does he need to stand there? I mean, adjacent to my earhole? Doesn't do a lot for concentration does it? Excuse me, son —

JANE.   He isn't altogether bright.

STAGG *(to TURK)*.   Could you — *(he gestures)* — over there a bit?

JANE.   He isn't a hundred per cent.

STAGG.   No, but he can understand plain English, can't he? Don't have to prod him with a stick. He is a human being, Jesus Christ. *(To TURK)* Just go over there a bit. *(TURK stares at him.)* Oh, come on, lad!

JANE *(to TURK)*.   Turk, would you kindly — *(She points)*. Thank you. *(TURK backs off to the far left.)*

STAGG.   You have the touch. He must like ladies. As I was rather gracelessly explaining —

TURK.   **Oh, thou great bollocking bum boy, thee!**

STAGG.   Naturally the enquiry will pay the utmost heed to your remarks —

COOPER.   You distrust us. You hold us in contempt.

STAGG.   Did I indicate that? I think that's running on a bit.

COOPER.   I read between the lines, Mr Stagg. It is the shortest way to the truth.

STAGG.   Well, that has the ring of wisdom, Colonel, but I doubt it has the substance. I will tell you what I do distrust. I distrust anyone who baulks at public scrutiny. I distrust a man who thinks his bank balance is a sacred temple or his tax return is more private than the pudenda of his wife. I have a saying, Cooper. If you have nothing to hide, don't shit yourself.

JANE.   I have something to say. May I say it?

STAGG. Don't spare me, Mrs Cooper.

JANE. Your manner is loathsome.

STAGG. Yes. Well, I expected something like that.

JANE. You come here like an enemy. And we are not your enemy. It is unnecessary, and worse, it is a lie. I don't understand it.

STAGG. I'm sorry I haven't the polish of your neighbours, Mrs Cooper. Frankly, I don't know a horse's arse from its ears.

JANE. I said it's a lie.

STAGG. For some reason etiquette was not included on the plumbing course.

JANE. Please, don't persist in the lie! *(Pause. He stares at her.)* When you know we are in this together. *(Pause.)*

STAGG. We are, are we? *(Pause.)*

COOPER. I'm on trial then. I'm to be publicly stripped.

STAGG. Well, I never said that.

COOPER. The shame squeezed out of me. Here stands a man burnt out of office. Here a mandarin who forced the slaves into revolt.

STAGG. These are all your captions. I am simply instituting business. Can we eat?

JANE. Who will do it?

STAGG *(making to go)*. Some minor civil servant. One for whom a knighthood is in prospect come retirement. We are being more intelligent with titles now. Mac manufacturers must get by with a plain esquire.

TURK *(seeing them move)*. Woon't dogs back, missus?

JANE. Yes, call them, Turk. *(He whistles loudly, musically.)*

STAGG *(looking into the distance)*. They won't let us build another prison on the moor. The climate causes chest diseases. I can see the D of E will have to rehabilitate the ruins and charge fifty p. Certainly they're picturesque. And black like that. A sort of Stonehenge erected to the God of Retribution, a pagan deity much respected by the public, I might add. You have strong feelings on reform now, Cooper, don't you? *(He turns. COOPER is weeping.)* Cooper?

JANE. Oh, Christ, you've made him cry.

STAGG. I have? *(Embarrassed silence. TURK whistles again.)*

TURK. Booger it! Bluddy animal's wrong side o't fence!

JANE *(to STAGG)*. Please don't fuss about it. *(She starts to go out.)* He'll catch up. The dogs, Turk! *(STAGG follows JANE out.)*

TURK. Tryin' missus! *(He whistles again, looks at* COOPER.*)* I have seen decay in men, but you are something special. You are lower than I hoped to see in my blackest moment. *(*COOPER *goes out, ignoring him.* TURK *looks across the moors for some moments.)* Turk, you are a very deep hole. You are an old black shaft with flowery brambles hanging on the rim. No sunlight strays more than an inch into a smile of yours . . . *(The dogs bark.)* **Eh, cum on, then, get me bum, ya bastards! Bite my arse!**

He charges out, waving the leads and yelling. Blackout.

Scene Three

The moors. Three people are standing gazing at the view. They are wearing macs and carry briefcases. Pause.

JARDINE. Forgot my fucking razor.

MATHESON. I'll get you one.

JARDINE. Fuck.

MATHESON. I said. I'll get you one.

JARDINE. Did you bring a razor, Mr Ponting?

PONTING. Yes, sir. A Philishave.

JARDINE. What is his name? I can't bear Ponting. Ye canna call a man Ponting all day.

PONTING. Barry, sir.

JARDINE. Barry Ponting. Jesus Christ.

PONTING. Lumbered.

JARDINE. Get it changed, son. There's no future in it.

PONTING. Yes, sir. Perhaps I could lend you my Philishave?

JARDINE. I did not ask ye if ye brought a piece of fucking clockwork, I asked if ye brought a razor.

PONTING. No, I didn't.

JARDINE. Christ, I am swearing a lot today.

MATHESON. You are. You have been swearing since we left Waterloo.

JARDINE. Never wanted to come here in the first place. Getting too old for this kind of thing. It's all right for young men. Hotels and Christ knows what in the arse ends of remoteness. I am sleeping rotten as it is. I will be seeing nuns in a minute.

PONTING. Nuns, sir?

MATHESON. Oh, do we have to go into that now?

JARDINE.   The nuns are a private matter. I should not have mentioned it.

MATHESON.   We're booked in at the Stagg's Arms.

JARDINE.   You mean the Stag's Head, Elizabeth.

MATHESON.   No, I mean the Stagg's Arms.

JARDINE.   Don't be fucking stupid, woman. How can a stag bear arms?

MATHESON.   Stagg was a landowner. Plutocrat as opposed to quadruped.

JARDINE *(pause)*.   The day you catch out Elizabeth, Mr Ponting — fucking hell, what are we going to call you — the day you catch out Miss Matheson, SMITH — it will be time to book her room in Bournemouth. She will be senile and in need of plastic drawers.

MATHESON.   Do you have to say things like that?

JARDINE.   I'm under no compulsion.

MATHESON.   I resent it.

JARDINE.   I note that.

MATHESON.   Please.

JARDINE.   I have said I note it.

MATHESON.   Talk to you later.

JARDINE.   Talk to me now.

MATHESON.   All right. Why do you find it necessary to make denigrating remarks about my sex? About incontinence and so on. Do you hate women?

JARDINE.   I doon't hate anybody.

MATHESON.   That is not an answer.

JARDINE.   You asked if I hated women. I said no. That is an answer. If it's not an answer I doon't know what is.

MATHESON.   Oh, God. . . !

JARDINE.   We are going to be in this forsaken place for Christ knows how many weeks. The fewer weeks the better, but some weeks for certain. I am not going to talk about incontinence, all right? I swear it. Fuck incontinence. Fuck everything. I have no bloody razor.

MATHESON.   I have said I will attend to that.

JARDINE.   Yes, I heard ye. *(He turns to* PONTING.) Well, Jim, this is a good start. Your first inquiry and everybody's bickering.

PONTING.   I expect they're always like it, Mr Jardine.

JARDINE. I wouldn't know. I haven't sat on one since 1970. That was in some fucking out of the way resort.

MATHESON. It was Brighton.

JARDINE. It was miles away and it was rotten.

MATHESON. It still is rotten. It is a criterion of rottenness. Corkscrew councillors. Cash coppers. A mayor who stank of fish.

JARDINE. I am for shooting 'em. When I joined the Communists I said what will you do with barrators and nepotists? They said shoot 'em. I said here's my subscription. Five years afterwards I asked again, what will you do with barrators and nepotists? They said re-educate 'em. I said have your card back. There is not enough education in the world, let alone re-education. I say shoot a man who abuses office. *(Pause.)* Mind you, I am an old man desperate for retirement. I will have my knight-hood and the pension, shan't I, Elizabeth, and run everywhere in the hope of dying quick.

MATHESON. I think we should book in. I sense one of the famous moorland mists.

JARDINE. The knighthood, Frank, says thank you. Thank you for plunging your arm down the gutter. It so happens that the silver smooth man kneeling to the royal hag in front of you is himself a money kisser, a puffball finance jobber with a pistol in the garden shed. Christ, England used to make me weep.

PONTING. Yes.

JARDINE. And it'll make you weep too, if you can stick it.

PONTING. Sir.

MATHESON *(moving away)*. What papers do we want at breakfast?

PONTING. I'd like the — *(He stops, for* JARDINE*)* Sorry, sir.

JARDINE. I'm not one for precedence.

PONTING. The Guardian.

JARDINE. Then you sit at your own table.

PONTING. Sorry?

MATHESON. Mr Jardine will not allow it in his presence. It is one of his peccadilloes.

PONTING *(brightly)*. Ah, the type-setting gets up your nose, sir?

JARDINE. Fuck the type-setting, old boy. It is the lethal odour that comes off the pages.

MATHESON *(gazing about)*. There really is one of these famous mists. I can't even see the prison. Shall we shift?

JARDINE.   Not till I've explained to John here why he won't be joining us at breakfast. If I had read that paper, Frank, I would have had the vision of a crate of scotch, bamboozled into thinking I was sharing decent thoughts with decent men, pissed crooked on my own fucking humanity. Know your enemies, old boy. Read the Express. *(Pause.)* Christ, I have mixed so many metaphors I — where in fuck's name are we?

MATHESON.   We are entirely cut off by the mist.

PONTING.   Came up like a —

MATHESON.   Thief.

PONTING.   Exactly.

JARDINE.   We shall have to cuddle up together, Elizabeth. We shall have to be intimate for the sake of warmth.

PONTING.   I think the idea in these situations is to find a sheep.

JARDINE.   A sheep! The boy is proposing buggery!

MATHESON.   This is Barry's first day with us. May I remind you.

JARDINE.   He can quit if he likes. I'm not stopping him. He'll be demoted quicker than he can swallow, but he can leave us if he wants. Do you not find my company congenial, old boy?

PONTING.   I hope I never gave that impression, Mr Jardine.

JARDINE.   You give me no impression whatsoever, Sammy. You are a man without a face, without a voice, without a cock for all I know.

MATHESON.   Oh, come off it George!

PONTING.   It's all right, Miss Matheson.

JARDINE.   I apologize. I am being billious.

MATHESON.   You bloody are.

JARDINE.   I have apologized.

MATHESON.   His name is Barry.

JARDINE.   Barry, I apologize.

PONTING.   Please, don't bother.

JARDINE.   Barry, Barry, old boy. Tell me something. What do you think we're doing here? *(Pause.)* Be quite honest with me. Be as abusive as you like. As rude and icono-fucking-clastic as you like. *(Pause.)* Let it rip. *(Pause.)*

PONTING.   Writing a report, Mr Jardine?

MATHESON *(who has sat down and is looking through a file).*   No. *(She looks up.)* No. That isn't what he wants.

PONTING.   Oh.

MATHESON.   Is it, George? Not really what you want. Mr Jardine wants you to take the piss out of it. Do you follow? Shit all over the job. And yet persist in doing it. It's a sort of grand machismo.

JARDINE.   Careful, Elizabeth.

MATHESON.   He is one of these people psychiatrists describe as partially complete. Only by abusing what he's doing can he extract the slightest satisfaction from it. Like a man who can't enter a woman unless he's poured vitriolic filth all over her. Called her a prostitute and so on.

JARDINE.   Elizabeth, you are being very stupid.

MATHESON.   He is a first-class civil servant but he will wallow in this self-contempt. I've put up with it for ten years and it is a spectacle of bloody impotence which you really needn't —

JARDINE *(flinging himself on her).*   **Jesus Christ I warned ye!**

MATHESON.   Don't hit me! **Do not hit me!**

JARDINE.   **Shut ye gob! Ye fucking harlot, will ye shut ye gob!** *(They roll over the turf, watched by an amazed and horrified* PONTING.*)*

PONTING.   Look here — listen — now, look! *(Sound of a whistle through the mist.)* Here. Over here!

The whistle blows again. WHIP *enters, in a long prison mac and holding a walking-stick. He stares at the spectacle.*

WHIP.   Christ, what's going on?

PONTING *(to his superiors).*   Will you stop it! Someone's here! *(They ignore him.* WHIP *bends down to them.)*

WHIP.   Pack it in yer silly buggers! *(He bends lower.)* Oi! *(They continue struggling.* WHIP *stands up, shaking his head.)* Who is it? Yer mum and dad?

PONTING.   Can you separate them, please?

WHIP.   I can't. I'm not a copper. Even if I was, I couldn't. Not if it's domestic, see?

PONTING *(boldly).*   **Mr Jardine, this is a disgrace!**

The struggle ceases. They both sit up. MATHESON *has a nose bleed.*

WHIP.   What did yer say? *(He looks at a piece of paper.)*

MATHESON.   I have a nose bleed.

WHIP.   Who did yer say?

MATHESON.   Barry, please give me a handkerchief.

JARDINE.   I apologize.

MATHESON.   Do you.

JARDINE.   I am a bastard.

WHIP.   Jardine, is it? *(MATHESON dabs her nose with PONTING's handkerchief.)* Oh, bleeding hell. *(He turns away to conceal a smirk, shaking his head.)*

JARDINE.   I am a fucking, obscene **bastard.** I have made her bleed. Elizabeth —

MATHESON.   **Don't touch me.**

JARDINE.   I am a loathsome, fucking animal.

MATHESON.   Do shut up.

JARDINE.   Forgive me, Elizabeth.

MATHESON.   Will I, fuck!

PONTING.   I think this gentleman is from the Prison.

WHIP.   I am looking for a Mr Jardine and his party. Which is you, I take it?

MATHESON *(rising to her feet).*   Thank you, yes.

WHIP.   I am Chief Officer Whip.

MATHESON.   I see. Can anybody see my bag?

PONTING.   The mist came down.

WHIP.   It does do.

MATHESON.   I am very sorry to have brought you out. *(She starts putting the files back in her case.)*

WHIP.   I love it. I am only sorry we no longer have the dogs. That was an exhibition, when we had the dogs. No bugger ever got off the moors when we had dogs.

JARDINE *(still seated).*   I'm not moving.

WHIP.   This would be Mr Jardine, I presume?

JARDINE.   You presume right, mister. And I am not moving until the lady accepts my apology.

MATHESON.   Come on. Don't be silly.

JARDINE.   Elizabeth.

MATHESON.   We'll go, shall we? *(They look at JARDINE, who is perfectly still.)*

WHIP.   Come on, sir, the lady's —

JARDINE.   **Do not come on sir, me! Do you know who I am?**

WHIP.   I think so, sir.

JARDINE.   No need to think when ye can be positive. I am Jardine. I hold my commission from the Queen.

WHIP.   Yes, sir.

JARDINE.   I am not to be moved on. I am not a common loiterer.

MATHESON.   I think everyone finds this embarrassing.

JARDINE.   It is in your power to put an end to it. *(Pause. She stares at him.)*

MATHESON.   Christ, you are so — **dishonest!** *(Pause. He is unmoved.)* I accept your bloody apology.

JARDINE *(getting up at once).*   Good. Show us to our quarters, Mr Whip. *(He picks up his own brief-case.)* D'ye drink whisky? I have a malt in my bag to still a riot.

WHIP.   I am teetotal, Mr Jardine, sir.

JARDINE.   Christ, they are putting angels in the gaols.

WHIP.   Not really, sir.

JARDINE.   No. Not really, Mr Whip. *(They drift out,* PONTING *last, hanging back.)*

PONTING.   God help us, I am going to get nothing out of this. Please let there be a waitress with a pair of tits.

He goes to follow. Blackout.

Scene Four

The shell of C Block. A table and chair. BLOON *is sitting typing with one finger.* DOCKERILL *is walking up and down with a sheaf of notes.*

DOCKERILL.   Traces — of — carbonized — dioxin — *(Painful typing.)* — of — carbonized — dioxin — *(Ditto.)* A constituent of benzine — benzine — approx — imately — thirty — milligrams — by weight — enmeshed in — enmeshed in — *(Ditto.)* — woollen fibres —

BLOON.   Want to go to the toilet.

DOCKERILL.   Would seem to indicate — to indicate — a source of combustion — not compatible —

BLOON.   Bursting Bladder Tortures Typist.

DOCKERILL.   In — compatible, make that. Incompatible — with neglect — or accident. Full stop. Full stop. The woollen fibres — by residue — by residue —

BLOON.   Piss Presses Pelvis Punishingly.

DOCKERILL. Show no admixture — no admixture — of artificial substances, e.g. polyester — e.g. polyester — as is practically universal — in woollen garment manufacture — currently.

BLOON. Servile Secretary Slavers After Slash!

DOCKERILL. Currently. We would submit, there — therefore — the inflammable material — at local source — at local source — to be a cardigan or pullover — a cardigan or pullover — of old — or of exclusive make —

BLOON *(rising to his feet).* Exasperated Expert Exits in Expectation of Expressive Ecstasy!

BLOON/DOCKERILL. **Piss off!**

BLOON *goes out.* DOCKERILL *sits at the machine and continues one-finger typing. After a little while,* UDY *comes in, prowling, hands behind his back. He wanders round* DOCKERILL *as he works.*

UDY. Once upon a time there were two little goldfish in a bowl. Round and round they swam, nibbling, bubbling, crapping, as fish do, and they were a right pair of narcissistic little snobs, under the misapprehension, as they were, that the bowl constituted the whole universe, and that all their fishy patter was the very height of polished wit, snuffling down their gills and mincing through the water like subaquatic intellectual poofs. It was an exhibition of piscine satisfaction, but alas, doomed not to last, as goldfish very rarely do. A pike in search of shelter came tapping at the glass with his big teeth. Panic seized the goldfish and they flapped their fins. Alas, in pikeland no great value was attached to wit. *(Pause.)* Get out. Her Majesty's Government wants your room. *(Pause.* DOCKERILL *completes a sentence.)*

DOCKERILL. Udy's Fables.

UDY. Mr Jardine has swum in. He is a Scotch bugger and he likes authority. **Shun!**

He stands smartly at attention as COOPER *comes in with* JARDINE, MATHESON, PONTING, WHIP *and* ANGELA, *a girl recorder. They spread out,* ANGELA *keeping to the back at all times.*

COOPER. This is C Hall, where the fire burnt most. The walls withstood the fever but the roof has blown. It was an architectural wonder, spanning four hundred feet. When it burst the angry glass sprang down at us. Firemen cowered behind their pumps. Young soldiers imagined they were in a war.

MATHESON. Was there much overcrowding here?

COOPER. There were three to a cell. Isn't that right, Mr Whip?

WHIP. Three, sir.

COOPER. That is overcrowding, I daresay.

JARDINE. Everything I ask is unofficial, you understand that, Cooper. When it is official, I will say so, and Angela will note it. All that is official goes through Angela. *(She grins sheepishly.)* In half a dozen words, what is your view of punishment?

COOPER. That is too steep.

JARDINE. I am steep, aren't I, Miss Matheson? I have a reputation to keep up. *(He walks a little way ahead.)* The hotel beds are frightful, by the way. Have you endured the Stagg's Arms, Mr Udy?

UDY. I have not, sir. The saloon bar is like the buffet on the Auschwitz Express.

JARDINE. The bed I have is more suitable to a camel seeking accommodation for its humps. Two pits lined with jagged springs and the usual piss-stained ticking. When I turn I rouse the passions of the last century. Well, Mr Cooper, have you come up with anything?

COOPER. If I must.

JARDINE. Well, I hate must.

COOPER. Sin masquerading as Holiness. *(Pause.* JARDINE *weighs it.)*

JARDINE. Christ, Colonel, you have me there. Two words to spare as well. I shall have to ponder that one, shan't I, Angela, over the soggy breakfast cereal. *(She grins sheepishly.)* What about you, Mr Udy? Punishment in half a dozen words?

UDY. Got to have it, haven't you?

JARDINE. That's crisp. And not so hollow as it seems.

COOPER. What about you, Mr Jardine? No doubt the calcinated suffering of this place inspires you? *(Pause.* JARDINE *looks at* COOPER.*)*

JARDINE. I am for it. *(Pause. He turns away.)* Well, I like this place, and I like to set my throne bang in the middle of the premises. When I did the Sinking Motorway Inquiry in the 60s I cross-examined underneath the flyovers. The knowledge they were standing under the products of their skimped workmanship did wonders for the contractors' evidence.

MATHESON. There is no roof on it.

JARDINE. It can't be beyond the prison service to get something rigged.

PONTING. Heating, Mr Jardine.

JARDINE. Paraffin, Ponting.

BLOON *returns from the lavatory.*

BLOON. Oh, sorry, is —

DOCKERILL. We are about to be dislodged.

COOPER.   These gentlemen are the Fire Inspectorate.

UDY.   They are on their way, sir.

JARDINE.   Which hotel are you in?

BLOON/DOCKERILL.   Mrs — *(Pause.)*

DOCKERILL.   Mrs Ackroyd's B & B.

JARDINE.   It sounds a nest of comfort.

BLOON.   If you like nylon sheets and pillowcases.

JARDINE.   Old boy, it wouldn't come between me and a good night's kip.

DOCKERILL.   Burning nylon gives off a very toxic fume.

BLOON.   Mrs Ackroyd's hasn't got a fire certificate. But then neither has the Stagg's. No one has in Middenhurst.

DOCKERILL.   We plotted shortest exits in both establishments. The Stagg's is a potential death-trap. They have linen sheets but no flame doors.

JARDINE.   You are a pair of butterflies. All your expertise must make it very difficult to settle.

DOCKERILL.   One shouldn't mock fire, Mr Jardine. It does terrible things to bodies. I once saw the official German documents on Dresden. For this I had to sign in six different places. The photographs would stagger you.

JARDINE.   Yes. We sent a letter to the Germans inviting them to surrender. But they wouldn't. *(Pause.)*

MATHESON.   What is that supposed to mean?

JARDINE *(moving to middle).*   I will have my table here. Across the middle, Mr Whip.

MATHESON.   What exactly are you saying?

JARDINE.   And I have a chair from London, my own official chair, worn to the contours of my bum.

MATHESON.   Would you explain? George?

JARDINE.   It is to be collected from the station.

MATHESON.   **Will you not ignore me.** *(Pause.)* **Please!**

Pause. JARDINE *looks at her.*

COOPER.   I think what Mr Jardine meant was that confronted with barbarity, with an excessive, utterly deformed brutality that clamps on every weakness and spits your bleeding charity into your face, confronted with a baked cynicism that interprets every gesture of redemption, every hint of reclamation as a pandering effeminacy and every smile as evidence of secret shame, that screams your civilization to the rafters in a torrent of abuse, there is but one response. Against such petrified hostility as this, all decency, though you hold it as your banner, has no voice. All the fire becomes . . . is proper . . . though it fall on guilty and innocent alike . . . *(Pause. They are all looking at him.* WHIP *and* UDY *with a mutual glance.)*

JARDINE. You paraphrase me very well.

MATHESON. If you can't win 'em, burn 'em. The Book at Bedtime is the Old Testament down here, I see.

JARDINE *(turns away to* WHIP.*)* Mr Ponting is in charge of practical arrangements, among other things. I believe his bedroom is even more liable to spontaneous combustion than my own, so consult him quickly, please. *(He looks to* COOPER.*)* Colonel Cooper, shall we proceed? *(They start to lead off, then* JARDINE *stops, turns to* DOCKERILL *and* BLOON.*)* I am sorry to disrupt you, gentlemen. I am avid for your report. I only hope you write good English. *(He starts to move again, and his train).* Three copies, please, then fifteen others for the records. There are miles of steel-lined tunnels under Berkshire waiting for your papers. That's our grip on immortality

He goes out, followed by all but PONTING, *who hangs back, with a note-book, jotting.* DOCKERILL *puts the lid on the typewriter.* BLOON, *with an air of resignation, collects up the papers.*

PONTING. Say what you like in front of me. *(They ignore him.)* I am only dogsbody. *(They just work on, stuffing papers in bags.)* They were scrapping earlier. Fists and so on. Made her bleed. *(Pause.)* Has to do with sex, of course. *(Pause. He walks, jotting as he goes.)* Which I am not exactly overburdened with. Are you? *(Pause.)* **Middenhurst, Copulation Capital of Britain, Folks!** Middenheap, more like it. What's the beer like?

BLOON. We don't drink.

PONTING. 'Ello, 'ello, wot 'ave we 'ere! Don't drink?

DOCKERILL. That's what he said.

PONTING. Fair enough. *(Pause.* DOCKERILL *puts on his jacket.)* Look, can we just forget all that? Sorry. The beer patter and what not. That is just — can we start again? *(They look at him, puzzled.)* I am rather shy of people and I tend to fall back on that sex and beer stuff. *(Pause.)* I can't stand beer myself. *(Pause.)* I was at Cambridge, in a rather tenth-rate college and beer was the lingua franca. *(Pause.)* Fuck beer. *(He looks up, at last.)* Can I lend you a hand?

BLOON. No thanks.

They go out, cases bulging with papers and typewriter under DOCKERILL's *arm.* PONTING *watches them leave. Pause.*

PONTING *(addressing the sky)*.   **Don't ignore me! I am not to be ignored.**
  (Pause. WHIP *comes in.)*

WHIP.   Ah. You're still here. Mr Jardine says to get along.

PONTING *(adjusting his tie)*.   Thank you.

He goes out. WHIP *watches him leave, then with a rapid glance over his
shoulder, lets down his trousers and squats. He is deep in concentration when*
TURK *appears, pushing his broom.* WHIP *leaps up.*

TURK.   Sorry, Mr Whip.

WHIP.   Made me jump, you bastard.

TURK.   Sorry. *(Cautiously,* WHIP *reasserts his posture.* TURK *watches.)*
  What yer doin', Mr Whip?

WHIP.   What do you think, you silly bastard. Look out there. See no one's
  coming. *(*WHIP *just stares.)* Did you 'ear! *(*TURK *turns, goes to the left,
  watches.* WHIP *strains.)* Bugger. Upset me. Bugger it. *(Pause.)* Christ,
  you'd think there was a better way of —

TURK.   No one coming, Mr Whip.

WHIP.   Wha'! *(He jumps up again.)*

TURK.   No one coming, Mr Whip. *(Pause, then* WHIP *abandons the
  project, pulls up his trousers.)*

WHIP.   Do you find it funny, Turk, that a man of authority should
  condescend to shit in front of you?

TURK.   Should what, Mr Whip?

WHIP.   Should show his whatnots to a con? Does that strike you as odd at
  all?

TURK.   No, sir.

WHIP.   Not odd? **Flashing his chopper** with you there? Well, I'll tell you
  why I am able to do it, shall I? Because my hairy, doggy fundament does
  not regard you as a human being. That's why. Because it feels the same
  embarrassment in front of you as it does with the toilet pan. So what does
  that make you, Turk?

TURK.   Sorry, sorry, Mr Whip, I —

WHIP.   It makes you **what**? *(*TURK *shrugs.)* It makes you a toilet pan.
  Say it.

TURK.   Toilet pan. *(Pause.)*

WHIP.   You'd say anything, wouldn't you?

TURK.   Yes, Mr Whip.

WHIP.   Water off a duck's back, eh?

TURK.   Sir.

WHIP. **Is it though!** *(Pause. He goes very close to* TURK *.)* I know you, Turk. I know you hate me, and I know it hurts.

TURK. Sir?

WHIP. Sticks and stones may break my bones, but names will never hurt me. **Bollocks.** *(Pause, he stands back, walks a little, stops.)* There was this very hot place I went to once. It was the hottest place in the world. That is a fact. It's in the Guinness Book of Records. It was called Crater. It may still be Crater for all I know, the People's Republic of Crater or some bollocks, I expect. It was a pile of blazing white clay hovels and it was full of terrorists. We didn't have a presence there. It wasn't diplomatic, some monkey in Westminster said. But our C.O. was funny. We had this kinky notion we should be killing terrorists. So we went in, to make 'em fight, behind a piper in a kilt. This piper, bouncing in a landrover, bringing his weird and horrible music right into the secret places of these lurking wogs, to provoke 'em, but they wouldn't fight. They stared at us with eyes not unlike yours. The eyes speak, don't they, Joseph? And we jumped down and stood 'em up against the baking walls, and we abused 'em, we coughed out every filthy phrase we'd ever learned. There are only so many filthy words, you know. Very few when it comes down to it. Most frustrating, we kept having to come back to fuck. And some of 'em, although they didn't cop the meaning, knew what we were doing to their pride, and their eyes streamed tears, bayonets tickling their arses all the time. I never knew the power of abuse until I went to Crater. I never knew how it could bring men down. You never cry, Turk, but you hurt inside.

TURK. Gotta sweep up, Mr Whip. *(Pause. They stare at each other.)*

BLOON. Not stopping yer. *(*TURK *begins pushing the broom round the hall.)* I am, as a matter of fact, not a very brave man. I am nothing very wonderful.

TURK. Dunno, sir.

WHIP. Dunno, sir! It used to be a saying here, Udy was a gent, but Whip's a bitch's bastard.

TURK. Never 'eard that, Mr Whip.

WHIP. No, of course. *(Pause.)* Turk, if anybody asks, I was all right to you. You hear? *(Pause.)* Don't sweep when I'm talking! *(*TURK *stops.)* I said if anybody asks, I was all right to you.

TURK. Who's gonna ask me, Mr Whip?

WHIP. Christ knows. But there will be lots of nasty words in circulation. Words like sadist. They will try to stick the word on me. You tell 'em different if they ask you. You stick up for me.

TURK. Okay, Mr Whip.

WHIP. Mr Whip a sadist? Never. Say that. *(Pause.)* Go on, say it!

TURK.   Mr Whip a sadist — wha'?

WHIP.   Never.

TURK.   Never.

WHIP.   That's it.

TURK.   What is a sadist, Mr Whip?

WHIP.   Never mind what it is. I am not one. *(He starts to walk away, stops.)* I am rather a shy man, actually. I have very little confidence. That is why at odd times, I have to be so mean to you. *(TURK just gawps.)* Don't mean anything to you, that, does it? Too psychological? There were geezers here who caught live mice and skinned 'em. Same thing. *(TURK just looks.)* I dunno why I waste my breath on you.

He goes out. TURK watches him go. Fade to black.

Scene Five

C Hall, laid out for the inquiry, i.e. a single chair faces a row of three tables, behind which are chairs for JARDINE, MATHESON *and* PONTING. *A small desk and chair, separated from the rest, ready for the shorthand recorder. It is 8 a.m.* JARDINE *is standing in the middle of the space, holding a bottle of Glenlivet.*

JARDINE.   Ye wanna know what I have in my pocket. I will tell ye. I have the **Queen** here in my pocket, an' if ye don't believe me you can have a little look. Only a little look, mind you. Only a teeny, weeny little look. Ready? *(He tears open the front of his jacket and closes it again.)* **Whassat!** *(Pause.)* It's a **Queen,** that is. I canna show ye too long because she is a r – r – retiring woman. I mean, she is no fucking **exhibitionist,** is she? She is no queen for masturbators. She is a queen for people of **good taste.** (PONTING *appears, holding a clock and a box of pencils.* JARDINE *does not see him.)* And I need not tell ye that the English people are not fuckin' short on taste. They have The Guardian, and they have Queen Elizabeth, and ye can no ask more of human wit and ingenuity than that. I say that as a fucking patriot. I say that as an ex-fucking Communist. So when ye talk to me, ye're no talking to me at all, it is **Elizabeth Alexandra Mary Windsor Saxe Fucking Coburg Battenberg** ye're talking to. Her warrant of commission — *(He taps his inside pocket.)* I carry here, against my heart. *(He staggers slightly. Pause.)*

PONTING.   It's Ponting, sir.

JARDINE.   Ponting.

PONTING.   Start in fifteen minutes, sir. *(He holds up the clock.)* Put the clock here, shall I? All right here? *(He stands it on* JARDINE's *desk.)*

JARDINE.   Ponting.

PONTING.   Sir?

JARDINE *(beckoning him closer)*.   Ye will have noticed I am after Matheson.

PONTING.   Sir?

JARDINE.   Christ, I am no fucking inaudible, am I?

PONTING.   I meant, really, are you?

JARDINE.   I really am. And the fact is, I am not well-educated in the mysteries of the female sex, old boy. I am sixty-three but I have been no fingerer of skirts. I cannot spew out the charm at oily little bistros, see? I am no candle-lighter, are ye with me?

PONTING.   Yes.

JARDINE.   I have been with my wife and I have been with prostitutes. As for my wife, old boy, I have had many years of satisfaction from her, and likewise in return, I daresay. She happens to prefer a rose called Marshal Foch to my attentions now, and I don't blame her. Thirty years is a long time in the same socket. Good luck to Marshal Foch and all who cultivate him, but I must get together with Matheson, Ponting, I am no for roses yet.

PONTING.   I see.

JARDINE.   What's your advice?

PONTING.   **My** advice?

JARDINE.   Christ, he is a fucking parrot. I shall have to call him Polly.

PONTING.   Mr Jardine, we have only got ten minutes left.

JARDINE.   I saw ye talking to the waitress this morning. What did ye say to her?

PONTING.   Waitress?

JARDINE.   There he goes again.

PONTING.   Waitress?

JARDINE.   **Ye were chatting up the waitress, Jesus Christ!** *(Pause.)*

PONTING.   Oh, that.

JARDINE.   On the way out the dining room. Ye stopped. I saw ye. She burst out laughing at your wit. I am not a blind man, Polly.

PONTING.   Yes. Well, I wanted to ask her something.

JARDINE.   Ye're a smooth operator, Mr. Ponting. I asked ye what ye said to her. To make her laugh like that. *(Pause.)*

PONTING.   I asked her for some All Bran. *(Pause.)* And she said I would have to buy my own. It's a rotten hotel, isn't it?

He walks away and starts laying the pencils at the desks. MATHESON *comes in with* ANGELA.

MATHESON.   Good morning.

ANGELA *(primly, going directly to her desk)*.   Good morning.

JARDINE.   I have been here since half-past-six.

MATHESON *(sitting at her place)*.   Yes, well you always are, aren't you, on the first day?

JARDINE.   I have been pacing up and down the melancholy hall. Treading the flags like a condemned man. You are here for a little month or two, Angela. Imagine it were several years.

ANGELA *(at her desk)*.   'Orrible.

JARDINE.   She says horrible.

MATHESON.   It was arson, then? I was reading till my eyes gave out.

JARDINE.   It was arson.

MATHESON *(organizing her desk)*.   And we are taking the warders first?

PONTING.   Strictly speaking, they are not warders. The proper name is prison officer.

JARDINE.   Strictly speaking, I do not care if they have turnkey painted on their arses.

PONTING.   Me neither, but —

JARDINE.   They think by giving a new name to an old complaint they will take the sting out of it. The Ministry of War is the Ministry of Defence. A rubber bullet is a Civil Authority Auxiliary. I hear they are planning to call cancer Libra. My belly won't be fooled by that.

The alarm clock rings. They all look at it. PONTING *switches it off.*

PONTING.   Shall I get the first man in?

JARDINE.   Mr Ponting, I am no a stickler for formality, I tell ye that. I am no for hiding behind a white shirt and a college tie that glistens when the sunshine catches it. You will notice that my tie has egg stains on it.

PONTING.   Sir.

JARDINE *(pointing)*.   Observe the egg stain.

PONTING.   Sir.

JARDINE.   Remember it.

PONTING *(seriously)*.   Right.

JARDINE.   All right. Get him in. *(PONTING goes out.* JARDINE *leans back in his chair, the whisky bottle in front of him.* MATHESON *taps a pencil nervously on her desk.)* I heard ye washing this morning. Your sink is against my wall.

MATHESON.   I was up early to finish the report.

JARDINE.   I had forgotten how erotic it is to hear a woman washing. *(Pause.)*

MATHESON.   I heard you drop your false teeth in the glass last night.

JARDINE.   Oh, good. We have both been thrilled, then.

Pause, then with a clatter of boots, UDY *comes in, stands before the desks and salutes crisply.*

UDY.   Senior Officer Udy, sir!

JARDINE.   Oh, thank you. You salute very well. I was in the army four years but I never got to salute like that.

UDY.   It needs a lot of practice, sir.

JARDINE.   I did practise. It must have something to do with the arm, do ye think?

UDY.   I have a good arm, Mr Jardine.

JARDINE.   You would need one in a place like this.

UDY.   Has the inquiry commenced, sir, please? Or is this a pleasantry? I would remind you I am not on oath.

JARDINE.   No, Mr Udy, and ye never will be. Not while I conduct things here.

UDY.   No oath, sir?

JARDINE.   That's what I said.

UDY.   Then how can you rely on my evidence, sir?

JARDINE.   Because I ask you. I would give it no more credence because you prefaced it with God, the Queen and all the angels, than if ye did so with the brand name on your girlfriend's knickers.

UDY.   I take the point. Only I was under the impression it was mandatory.

JARDINE.   Do not joust with me, Mr Udy, I am not a mandatory man.

UDY.   As you wish, sir.

JARDINE.   That's very good of ye. Mr Ponting has some questions. *(Pause.* PONTING *looks horrorstruck.)*

PONTING.   No — I — er — I don't think —

MATHESON.   Mr Ponting has not prepared questions for this witness.

JARDINE.   Make some up, then. Udy here will think we are a shambles.

MATHESON.   Mr Ponting has never examined a witness.

JARDINE.   There is a first time for all of us. There was a first time Udy had to stop a fight. Isn't that right, Udy? I bet your heart was thumping.

UDY.   Correct, sir.

JARDINE.   Well, Mr Ponting's baptism is a wormlike thing compared to that. *(Pause. He leans back in his chair gazing at the high walls while* PONTING *fumbles.)* It's a funny thing. I have noticed how the sun never comes in these windows.

UDY.   No, sir. They laid the prison East to West.

JARDINE.   Ye could no take deprivation much further than that.

UDY.   You could, sir.

JARDINE.   How's that?

UDY.   Have no windows at all. We had a special row called Problem Block. It was for the awkward and determined. It had no windows. It was concrete on six sides. Colonel Cooper did away with that.

JARDINE *(turning to* PONTING *).*   Mr Ponting, there is a ledge for your fingers to get a catch.

PONTING.   I'm just — I'm thinking I —

JARDINE.   You are fucking slow to frame a question. I could have written a novel in the time it's taken you to put the date.

UDY.   This is so informal, isn't it? Incredible.

PONTING *(standing, with his pencil).*   How would you describe the atmosphere at Middenhurst, Mr Udy?

UDY.   The atmosphere?

PONTING.   Yes. *(Pause.)*

UDY.   Good.

PONTING.   Thank you. *(He jots it down, looks up.)* Before the fire broke out, was there any sign of discontent?

UDY.   Discontent?

PONTING.   Yes.

UDY.   No, sir.

PONTING.   Thank you. *(He jots this down, hesitates.)* No rioting? Nothing like that?

UDY.   **Rioting?**

PONTING.   Yes. You know — people — running about?

UDY.   **Running about?**

PONTING.   Yes *(*UDY *shakes his head contemptuously.)* No? *(*UDY *shakes again.)* That means no, does it?

JARDINE.   I think Mr Udy is getting the better of you, Mr Ponting. Mr Udy has been in front of inquiries half a dozen times before. He is very deft at repeating your phrases back to you.

UDY.   Answer the questions, sir. Can't do more than that.

PONTING.   Yes, but do you? *(Pause.* UDY *looks cruelly at him.)* Answer the questions? *(Pause.)* You see, I think you are lying. I think there was a lot of discontent.

UDY *(to* JARDINE*).*   I am not to be called a liar, am I?

PONTING.   We will have the truth now, Udy, please.

UDY.   Excuse me. I have been called a liar.

PONTING.   Yes. And I repeat it.

JARDINE.   Mr Ponting, I'm sure I enjoy Perry Mason every bit as much as you, but we are in England, and in England you may think a man a liar but you are better not to call him one. That is called maturity. The more mature you are, the less you use the word you want. The purpose of wrapping meanings up in cotton-wool is to stop them hurting. This is a very sick and bandaged race.

UDY.   Am I entitled to an apology?

JARDINE.   You may well be, Mr Udy. And it costs nothing, does it? Mr Ponting will probably oblige.

PONTING *(sitting).*   Beg pardon.

UDY.   Accepted with good grace. You're new to this.

JARDINE.   Now, Mr Udy, how would you describe the atmosphere at Middenhurst?

UDY.   As I just indicated, it was good.

JARDINE.   Good. A good fight. A good fuck. A good apple.

UDY.   You are indicating the absence of validity in the word good. I am a bit of a philosopher myself. *Principia Ethica* was on the reading list for my language class. I have thirty copies, still in mint condition, I regret to say.

JARDINE.   Mr Udy, you follow me. What about this atmosphere? *(Pause.* UDY *draws himself up.)*

UDY.   The prision was well-run. There was a friendly and congenial relationship between the prisoners and the staff. Bearing in mind the deprivations to which incarcerated men are naturally subject, Middenhurst was a very happy place. *(He smiles.)* All right? *(Pause.)*

JARDINE.   Miss Matheson will question you. *(Pause.)*

MATHESON.   What is 'roughousing'?

UDY.   It is a practice, I believe. Not practised here, though.

MATHESON.   Describe it, would you?

UDY.   I can't with any accuracy because I've never witnessed one.

MATHESON.   Be inaccurate, then.

UDY.   A number of officers give a prisoner a rather unpleasant time. *(Pause.)* I gather.

MATHESON.   Why does it occur?

UDY.   Why is the sea blue?

MATHESON.   A combination of algaeic matter and depth.

UDY.   All right. Because tempers get a little rough.

MATHESON.   But there are procedures, are there not?

UDY.   There are indeed.

MATHESON.   And proper punishments?

UDY.   Absolutely.

MATHESON.   So why do tempers get a little rough?

UDY.   I can only suggest, since I have neither seen nor participated in a 'roughouse', as you call it, that individuals mistakenly believe the official method is inadequate. I guess, of course.

MATHESON.   Why do they seem inadequate?

UDY.   I can't imagine. They seem absolutely right to me.

MATHESON.   Too lenient, perhaps?

UDY.   Well, I don't know.

MATHESON.   Silly intellectuals' ideas, a little bit remote from struggles on the landings?

UDY.   Struggles on the landings? You must have read a book.

MATHESON.   Don't try to belittle me.

UDY.   Sorry.

MATHESON.   Struggles on the landings, I repeat?

UDY.   Not here, Miss. It is Miss, is it? *(Pause.)*

MATHESON.   I think you paint Middenhurst too rosy, Mr Udy.

UDY.   It is rather a rosy place. I say that despite the lack of interest in my language class. *(Pause.)*

MATHESON.   Someone set light to the prison. Can you think why?

UDY.   It baffles me.

MATHESON.   And when you saw the ruins, how did you react?

UDY.   I thought, that's a bit of Old England you won't see again. *(Pause.)*

MATHESON. All right.

UDY *(to* JARDINE*)*.   Is that all, sir?

JARDINE.   Udy — *(He gets up, slips a moment.)* Jesus Christ, I am half cut, and that's a fact — Udy — I must tell you, I have not heard in all my years as a winkler-out of truths, such a pig's bladder full of drivel as you have treated us to here this morning, old boy. It is an example of evasion such as would do credit to the chairman of a secondary bank at an emergency meeting of the shareholders. You belong in the City, old boy. You are wasted here. Why are you a gaoler? It can't be pity for the sinner that brings you here. *(Pause.)*

UDY.   I like the life.

JARDINE.   You like authority. Me too. *(Pause. He looks at him a moment, then waves his arm.)* Out, Udy. Out.

UDY.   Thank you, sir.

JARDINE.   Before ye go — *(*UDY *stops.)* let me tell ye something. The trick with inquiries is to give a little, but nothing very much. Give 'em the impression they have winkled something out. It makes 'em feel they are squatting on their slack old rims for some public purpose. You have come in here as smooth as aluminium and you're leaving the same way. You have aroused suspicion when you might have set us quacking with futile delight. For all your experience, you're a bloody fool. All right, Udy?

UDY.   Sir.

JARDINE *(sitting)*.   See you again, no doubt. *(*UDY *salutes, goes out. Pause.* JARDINE *is still, the rest wait.)*

PONTING.   Sir? *(*JARDINE *looks at him.)* Can I grill the next one, sir? I rather like it, actually. Only I think I was a bit too soft. *(*JARDINE *looks at him, then at* MATHESON.*)*

JARDINE.   I have been thinking of your stockings, Elizabeth.

MATHESON.   They come from Marks and Spencers. I will get you a pair if you like.

JARDINE.   I sat next to a girl in green stockings once. Upstairs on a 137 bus. It was in the sixties, when girls showed their arses when walking and when they sat next to you, you could feel the sweet breath of their private places on your hand. I held my bus ticket so that it touched her thigh, the full extent of which was visible to me, even to the light, fair hairs that got through the stocking, and the slightly goosey flesh that women have there. I was an old man to her. I was an old man to myself, for that matter. And as the bus jolted down Whitehall, my flimsy ticket jostled her . . . *(Pause.)* It was a pathetic sight, no doubt.

MATHESON.   No doubt.

JARDINE.   Have you ever had sex through a bus ticket, Ponting?

PONTING *(writing busily, unaware of this story).* No, sir. *(He looks at both* JARDINE *and* MATHESON, *keenly)* I thought I would come down like a ton of bricks on the first wriggle he makes. Rather than let him lie too much. I think terror straight away. I'm sure they squeal if you disorientate them on the first question.

JARDINE. Everybody has his methods. There is electricity, too.

PONTING. Electricity?

JARDINE. Attach it to their bollocks. *(PONTING sniggers briefly.)*

MATHESON. Not funny.

PONTING. No, of course.

MATHESON. Mr Jardine would not scruple at taping things to people's testicles. He has said so.

JARDINE. Or vaginas. I am no sexist.

PONTING. The next person is Chief Officer Whip.

MATHESON. He has said so, and yet he scuffles with the police outside the Chilean Embassy to emphasize his opposition to interrogation by electricity.

JARDINE. I am afraid, Elizabeth, the human race cannot yet afford the Absolute. Absolute pacifism. Bollocks. Absolute Truth. Bollocks. If a man had put a time-bomb in a classroom and would not tell us in which school it was, I would put radium up his arse hole.

MATHESON. Unless the children were paid-up members of the Junior Nazis, I suppose.

JARDINE. Ye see, there is no Absolute. *(To* PONTING.*)* Get Mr Whip in. If he is as smooth as Mr Udy, we shall be in this dump till Christmas. *(PONTING eagerly goes out.)* I admire you, Elizabeth, ye know that. Every year I write it on your birthday card. *(Pause.)* This year I shall be writing something else. *(ANGELA coughs.)* Don't mind us, Angela! I don't mind you. *(She laughs weakly.* PONTING *follows* WHIP *into the hall.)*

PONTING. Chief Prison Officer Whip.

WHIP *(saluting, not very smartly).* Whip, Michael Tudor, sir.

JARDINE. Tudor Whip? You sound like Henry VIII's afters, mister.

WHIP. Sir?

PONTING. Shall I start, Mr Jardine?

JARDINE. I would not want to hold you back, Ponting. You might kick down the stable door. *(Pause.* PONTING *stares at* WHIP *a moment.)*

PONTING. Mr Udy tells us things were getting out of hand in Midden-hurst. What do you say to that?

MATHESON *(appalled)*.   Just a minute —

PONTING.   Is that true, Whip?

MATHESON.   No. Just a minute. Angela, stop, please. *(She looks to* JARDINE*)* We can't have this. (JARDINE *looks.)* Can we? Mr Ponting can't do this. *(Pause.)*

JARDINE.   Whip, I'm afraid you've been misled. Mr Ponting will have another shot at it. *(Pause.)*

PONTING.   Whip, how were things in Middenhurst?

WHIP *(pause, he shrugs)*.   Getting out of hand, I s'pose . . .

MATHESON   *(standing)*. Stop, please, Angela. *(She looks to* JARDINE.*)* This is unethical.

PONTING.   In what way, Whip?

MATHESON.   Mr Ponting, we cannot proceed on the basis of —

JARDINE.   Will you put a sock in it? For Christ's sake let the witness speak. *(He looks to* ANGELA.*)* Angela, get on.

MATHESON.   I am withdrawing.

JARDINE.   Withdraw then. I'm no stopping ye. *(She collects up a file or two.)* Go to the toilet. Powder yer nose. *(She sits again.)*

MATHESON.   No, I'm not withdrawing.

JARDINE.   Christ, is she coming or going?

MATHESON.   I am entitled to be here!

JARDINE.   Certainly. It is your function.

MATHESON.   My function.

JARDINE.   Ye have a number of functions. Sitting next to me is one of them. There are others. Some of which are biological. Why ye do not carry them out is a matter for speculation —

MATHESON.   Oh, bloody hell —

JARDINE.   It is a mystery to the male sex what ye are so —

PONTING.   **I am cross-examining this man!** *(Pause. They both stare at* PONTING.*)* I am cross-examining this man. Please. Let me. *(Pause. He raises his eyes to* WHIP.*)* In what way were things getting out of hand. I think I asked you. *(Pause.)*

WHIP.   Just this an' that. (PONTING *leaves the desk, walks round* WHIP.*)* Now and again, you know.

PONTING.   This and that, now and again. You can do better than that. You are a Chief Officer, aren't you?

WHIP.   I'm sorry, I don't like inquiries.

PONTING.   It's nothing to me whether you like them or not.

WHIP.   I get so I —

PONTING.   You haven't told me anything.

WHIP.   No, well, I get so nervous —

PONTING.   I will make you very nervous if you don't speak up! *(Pause.)*

WHIP.   Trying to help.

PONTING.   Thank you. And I'm trying to help you. What went wrong here?

WHIP.   Colonel Cooper shut the Problem Block.

PONTING.   Go on.

WHIP.   We have some real bastards here. You have to have a Problem Block.

PONTING.   Or what? *(WHIP shrugs.)* Don't shrug at me! Or what?

WHIP.   Sorry?

PONTING.   Or what?

WHIP.   They run around.

PONTING.   And did they?

WHIP.   Yes. *(Pause.)*

PONTING.   Tell me what Cooper said.

WHIP.   What he said?

PONTING.   He has a theory, doesn't he? What is it?

WHIP.   A theory?

PONTING.   Look, if you just repeat my words back at me I shall think you are trying to be sarcastic —

WHIP.   I am not, sir.

PONTING.   I shall think you are belittling me.

WHIP.   I'm really not. I'm just — I am a bag of nerves, actually. I feel sick.

PONTING.   With nerves.

WHIP.   Yes, sir.

PONTING.   My heart bleeds for you. I asked you what the Governor thinks!

WHIP.   He said — he said — get it right —

PONTING.   Yes, get it right, Whip.

WHIP.   Give 'em their dignity. *(Pause.)* That's it.

PONTING. Their dignity.

WHIP. Give it to 'em, he said.

PONTING. And did you go along with that?

WHIP. Can I have a glass of water, please?

PONTING. No. Did you go along —

MATHESON. Of course he can have a glass of water.

PONTING. I am questioning him, please!

MATHESON. Mr Ponting —

PONTING. **He is not to have the water!**

MATHESON. Angela, give Mr Whip a —

PONTING. **He is using it! Can't you see he's using it!**

MATHESON. Mr Ponting.

PONTING. **Will you let me do this, please!** *(Pause.* PONTING *is white.)*

JARDINE. Sit down, Mr Ponting.

Pause, then PONTING *goes to his seat, sits with his face in his hands.* ANGELA *gives* WHIP *a glass of water.*

WHIP. Thank you. *(There is a pause.* JARDINE *looks at* WHIP.*)*

JARDINE. Ye see some strange things in this world, don't ye? Ye see how the mild-mannered Mr Ponting is a proper bastard when the wind catches him. How was Colonel Cooper, Tudor, when the wind caught him? *(*WHIP *shrugs.)* Was he ruining the gaol?

WHIP. In my opinion.

JARDINE. That's the one we're interested in.

WHIP *(shrugging).* Prisoners are like children. Bloody simple. Bloody rough. You wouldn't trust a baby with a boiling kettle, would you? Same with prisoners and liberty. *(Pause.)*

JARDINE. **Mr Whip, what's dignity?**

WHIP. I dunno. Frankly. I dunno.

JARDINE. You don't know.

WHIP. I couldn't put it into words. *(Pause.)* I was in Aden. At home they were saying, be nice to the blackies. In Parliament. But they had never walked down a street of 'em, had they? Same in 'ere.

JARDINE. Very easy from the Commons plush.

WHIP. We had a saying. When Labour MPs got off the benches they left black bumprints on the old red seats. *(Pause.)*

JARDINE.   How bad was it, then, Tudor?

WHIP.   We were up against it, sir.

JARDINE.   More fights? The weekly report shows thirty incidents in a single week.

WHIP.   We were getting assaulted. Horribly.

JARDINE.   Well, they were asserting their dignity, weren't they, Tudor? Ever been in another gaol like this?

WHIP.   No, sir. It was a piss-bucket of a place. *(Pause.)*

JARDINE.   Okay, Whip.

WHIP *(relieved)*.   Have you finished? Is that it?

JARDINE.   That's it. *(*WHIP *stands, is about to leave, stops.)*

WHIP.   Sir. Permission to say something?

JARDINE..   Speak freely, Mr Tudor Whip.

WHIP.   Someone's bound to say I was a sadist, sir. That's bound to come up, isn't it?

JARDINE.   And you would like me to remember that you weren't?

WHIP.   Sir.

JARDINE.   I will make a note of it. *(*WHIP *salutes, goes out.)*

PONTING.   Christ. . . !

MATHESON *(standing, looking to* JARDINE*)*.   Can I talk to you, please?

PONTING.   Oh, Christ. . . !

MATHESON.   Because there are rules governing the conduct of inquiries and we are gaily flouting them.

PONTING.   I think I may be very ill. *(He stands up, deathly pale.)*

JARDINE.   Go and get some fresh air, son. There are a thousand square miles of heather out there. Go and roll in it.

PONTING *(stopping on his way out)*.   I think I could be Himmler. I could have people squirming off of meat hooks. There is something very wrong with me.

JARDINE.   It's good to know what's crawling in your cavities. To lift the flowers and see what's wriggling underneath. It never hurt a man to see the insect that is in him. Unfortunately, Himmler fell in love with his . . . *(*PONTING *goes out.)*

'MATHESON.   You should not have let him cross-examine. We are always on the edge of illegality.

JARDINE.   No one has broken more rules than I have, or brought more plump little men to while away their last years in prison libraries, writing their memoirs while their widows weep in ranch-style, contract-fiddling bungalows. Don't wrap your rules round fat men's naked privates. I would have them hanging out, the better for a kicking. *(Pause. She looks at him.)*

MATHESON.   You are the most violent person I have ever met. I find you truly frightening.

JARDINE.   Yes. And yet I long for your comfort, Elizabeth. That is grotesque.

Fade to black.

Scene Six

The moors. PONTING, *breathless and in some disarray, runs on and flings himself to the ground, sobbing. After a few moments, he sits up and stares. Then, with manic decisiveness, he rips off his tie and starts strangling himself. After some futile seconds,* JANE *appears, holding the borzois' leads. She watches him.*

JANE.   The tie is Corpus Christi, isn't it? *(He looks up.)* Finis Opus Coronat?

PONTING.   Let me die, please.

JANE.   I knew a boy there once. A brilliant sculler.

PONTING.   I am going to be a burden on humanity, so I am doing the decent thing. Don't spoil a good intention, for Christ's sake.

JANE.   I often think of him, flicking the early morning water like a moorhen's wing, while behind the steamy college windows everybody lay asleep.

PONTING.   Please indulge your nostalgia somewhere else. *(Pause. She watches, he works at strangulation.)*

JANE.   It is impossible to kill yourself with a tie except by swallowing it. I know because I've tried it. Just when it begins to hurt they break. My husband's were Magdalene and Sandhurst but the material's the same, I would have thought.

PONTING.   **You are piling up agony for the human race!**

JANE.   Yes, no doubt, but I'm not very bothered about the human race. It deserves everything it gets, in my opinion. Anyway, what's so rotten about you? You look harmless enough. *(Pause, then* PONTING *begins sobbing again.)* Oh, what is happening to the male sex? You're not even menopausal. **Stop!** *(He looks up, stops. She walks a little way, gazes out over the moor.)* They say the White Man's grave is in West Africa. The White Woman's Grave is three hours out of Waterloo. I have dipped my forefinger in jars of skin cream in every hostile climate of the world, but I have never felt so old, so dry and so neglected as I have done here. My knees creak, and my hip grinds if I run. Not that I need to run. What is there to run for? *(She turns, sees that* PONTING, *still on his knees, has exposed himself. Pause.)* Ah. *(Pause.)* That hasn't happened to me since I was cycling in Penang. A Chinese in a rickshaw coming the other way . . . *(*PONTING *shuffles a little closer, slowly raises his hand towards her knee.)* I have to take the dogs back for their tea. *(She turns away.)*

PONTING.   Do I frighten you?

JANE.   Yes.

PONTING.   Good. Tell them the Beast of the Moor accosted you.

JANE.   All right. Can I go?

PONTING.   **Yes, go!** *(She goes out.* PONTING *is still, then zips up his fly.)* Oh, Mummy, you will have to take my picture off your wall. My baby shoes will make you weep more than ever now . . . *(He is suddenly aware of someone behind him. He stiffens.)*

TURK *(in yet another yokel dialect)*.   Kill yer if yer like it. Wuldn't know nowt of't. Jest say the word. *(Pause.)*

PONTING.   No thank you.

TURK.   Am an hixpert.

PONTING.   Really, I prefer to have a go myself.

TURK.   Hevn't got the knack, squire.

PONTING.   Look, this is supposed to be the remotest place in England. I would have had less interference if I'd disembowelled myself in Oxford Street!

TURK.   Wha' street's tha', zur?

PONTING.   Look, I don't need any help, thank you. *(*TURK *just looks at him.)*

TURK.   Yer from the governmint.

PONTING.   No.

TURK.   That tie. T'is governmint.

PONTING.   Forget the tie. I hate the tie.

TURK.   T'is governmint y'are.

PONTING.   **Was. Was** the government!

TURK.   The gear, squire —

PONTING *(ripping off his shirt and throwing it aside)*.   I have finished with the government! All right? Fuck government!

TURK *(watching this antic).*   Jesus, wh'ass 'appening to governmint?

PONTING.   Look, who are you?

TURK.   Jo Turk, zur. Killer. Seven year.

PONTING.   I see. *(Pause.)* Well, I don't require your services, thank you.

Pause. Then TURK *walks away a little, stops.*

TURK.   Can't live on moor, zur.

PONTING.   Can do. Can try. *(*TURK *stares at him.)*

TURK.   They have brought George Jardine in, to paste white paper on the sores. A dummy from the cabinet was seen flying by, muttering like the uncrowned king that something must be done. *(Pause.)* I took fire to their agonizing, mister, or I should have gone mad. *(Pause.)* I'll bring you food here if you're serious.

PONTING *(gawping).*   Christ, you're intelligent . . .

TURK.   Me, zur? *(Pause.)* Be cumming up wi' dogs tomorrer. See you, mebbe, shall A?

He goes out. Slow fade to black.

ACT TWO

Scene One

MATHESON *and* JANE *are together in the hall.*

JANE.   His body, one Malayan morning, one sunrise on Penang, in the sheet beside me, knees drawn up, arms clasping them, a foetal study alien to him, combat fatigues behind the door, lieutenant's pips on epaulettes, they had skirmished with guerillas and he had shot one, perfectly shot one through the eye not three hours earlier, and very tired, slept without touching me, slept awfully still and chastely, when I had been waiting, must admit it, waiting for him to come into me, had been all day thinking of this, but couldn't ask now, not after that, of course. There was so little doing in Malaya for an army wife. Of course I thought sex, newly married as I was, thought sex too much, but after shooting this man through the eye, how could I pester him? So he slept, his deep breath barely moving him, and I watched, telling myself you will have to wait, just wait. I thought of touching myself, but it seemed disloyal, when the colony was so full of treason.

MATHESON.   We were sitting in the garden in deck chairs. It was so hot you felt your skin actually turn. If you touched the secateurs you got a shock. High above us, the little silver specks of Flying Fortresses, silent on their way to Essen, Dortmund, Normandy perhaps. And lower, doodlebugs, in the opposite direction, very determined, very black, purring to plop on Croydon. We were witnessing an exchange of death in perfect luxury, him with tea and me with orange juice. I was twelve years old. I could not see why anything should ever interfere with that. I never got engaged. I never married. My father's dead. But I have never been really afraid of anything. If Hitler and the Americans could not change it, then what could? *(Pause.* MATHESON *looks out the window again.)* Your gardener's buttocks are so round.

JANE.   You could eat them.

MATHESON.   Oh yes, you could. You really could. *(Pause.)* Have you let him touch you?

JANE.   Touch me?

MATHESON.   Yes.

JANE.   I never thought of asking. It would not be fair, would it? I am the Governor's wife, and I owe it to him not to bring us in contempt.

MATHESON.   You are a very touchable person.

JANE.   And yet I go untouched. I once thought it extraordinary that women could go so long without it. Until I did myself. You forget why it exists. It doesn't knock against your legs like their thing, does it? Always reminding them.

MATHESON.   It bleeds, though.

JANE.   There was a time we wanted children. Every time it bled I loathed it. I sat weeping in the bathroom. Then I accepted it, that it would go on bleeding till I dried up. I even got to like it.

MATHESON.   Do you love him?

JANE.   He's honourable, and I've always rather fancied honourable men. It's become a fashion to like cheats, crooks and swindlers, but I got as much pleasure from his honour as a thief's tart from his thieving. I was a mannequin when mannequins existed. All the others wanted to be fucked by weight-lifters and blacks. I alone preferred English officers. *(Pause.)*

MATHESON.   Jardine has moved into the bedroom next to mine.

JANE.   Ah.

MATHESON.   And he's drinking. He is interpreting my not sleeping with him as an erotic manoeuvre. I have been with him ten years. For nine years he never looked at me. Then last year, as he puts it, he began to 'notice' me. Do you mind listening to this?

JANE.   I am loving talking to you.

MATHESON.   Me too. He thinks it effeminate to be romantic. His idea of considerate is to carry a handy box of Kleenex round with him. His latest concession to my feelings is that I should tell him when I want to fuck. When I refuse him he gets violent.

JANE.   There's violence and violence . . .

MATHESON.   He tries to strangle me. Which kind of violence is that?

JANE.   Apply for a transfer.

MATHESON.   I have done. I have filled the form in. Then I tore it up. He has integrity, and that gives him pain, pain that is actually rather beautiful to watch. He is simply vile to women.

JANE.   Do you like sex?

MATHESON.   No. Not much. Do you?

JANE.   I have done. But with every move we made I liked it less. I got an orgasm in Parkhurst once, when a child molester sang 'Jesu, Joy of Man's Desiring' in the Christmas concert. But the day we came to Middenhurst something gave out in me. We have been here two years and I have been as dead as a purse. I imagine I have finished.

MATHESON.   No one finishes.

JANE.   Oh yes, we do.

MATHESON.   The thing goes quiet, that's all.

JANE.   It dies.

MATHESON.   It is only flesh. It cannot die until you do.

JANE.   Mine died, I tell you. When it found itself in Middenhurst. It had its heyday in Malaya. It was at one with the vegetation. In this frozen, arthritic place it takes a cunt indeed to maintain any interest. *(Pause. MATHESON looks at her.)*

MATHESON.   I do like you. Why were you in Malaya?

JANE.   He was killing Communists. Later he ran a gaol in Nicosia. I carried a pistol during the Emergency. All the English women did. We got very trigger-happy. The locals were petrified of us. I shot a man once for carrying a loaf of bread. It looked like a sten-gun and he pointed it at me. You shouldn't make obscene gestures in a civil war. *(Pause.)*

MATHESON.   Your politics are to the right.

JANE.   To the right. *(Pause.)*

MATHESON.   Perhaps it's better if we just talk about our cunts. They say the rest is superficial. You wear such lovely clothes.

JANE.   It's the only benefit I can think of from having sheep as neighbours. You ought to buy something while you're here. They're expensive but they're unadulterated. Polyester might be democratic, but like democracy, you wouldn't wear it next to your skin. What are your politics? Are you a Liberal?

MATHESON.   I'm sure we can be intimate without knowing that. What we share as women is greater than what might separate us in our politics.

JANE.   I'm sorry, but I simply cannot talk cunt all the time. *(Pause.)*

MATHESON.   Very well. I am a Socialist. *(Pause.)*

JANE.   Then the only thing we have in common is the buttocks of the gardener.

MATHESON *goes out. Enter the officers, distraught.*

WHIP.   The Colonel is bananas! The loony has gone shrieking! Christ all bleeding mighty, someone lock the zoo!

UDY.   When he first came here I said, did I not, Michael, there is something in his eyes that makes me shrink. Those were my words. Something of the barmy which has bloomed. Look at his hands, shaking like a fucked bitch's tongue.

COOPER *(reappearing, jacketless and loosening his tie)*.   I was pillaged. I was ransacked. I was turned over like the corpse of Man's Worst Enemy. Had I been Hitler's coke remains I could not have been handled with less dignity!

JANE.   He has lost his man. Mr Barry Ponting, who hung out his thing to me, they are dragging the mire for. No wonder he is furious.

COOPER.   I was in Kuala Lumpur during the Chinese riots. White men's heads were footballs in the gutter. Under the torrent of this hatred, the superficial snobberies that split the English, healed as if by magic. They found a brotherhood matched only by the howling foreigner. We have got to find that spirit here. Jardine is an opium-crazed terrorist looking for a head to dribble.

UDY.   I said nothing, Colonel. I have learned the art of the inquiry. I have got the hang of it.

WHIP.   Me neither.

COOPER.   **Someone spoke!**

UDY.   Jardine —

COOPER.   **Opium-crazed —**

UDY.   As you wish. Opium-crazed Jardine has the figures. Maybe the weekly sheets have squealed on us.

COOPER.   This was our creation. This was our place.

UDY.   I'm not sure I fancy the ours very much. Do you, Michael?

WHIP.   Well . . .

UDY.   No, we don't.

JANE.   They're quitting you.

UDY. The Colonel and ourselves didn't see it eye to eye, Mrs. Nothing wrong with that, perhaps. Only when the razors came slashing, it was through our cheeks, not his. When riot wrecked the dining hall, the Colonel was choosing vintage in his cellar. We were quit, if anybody was.

JANE. You may not desert him.

WHIP. It's not a ship. The officers don't have to drown with it.

JANE. No matter what, there is a thing called loyalty.

WHIP. You have it, Mrs. You are his lady. *(Pause.)*

COOPER. What are you doing in my drawing room? *(The officers put on their caps, salute.)* You lance-corporals. How could I talk to your dull wits?

They withdraw. COOPER *stares out of the window.*

JANE. Talk to me now. *(Pause.)* You must do. *(Pause.)* I am your Jane. (COOPER *lets out a long, dull groan.*) I would give anything for us to talk. Try, please . . .

COOPER *(turning on her).* **What! What?**

JANE. I know, but try. *(Pause.)* I'm waiting . . .

COOPER. To open, even the emaciated shreds of conversation with you now, after this time, would take so long, and would produce so little, not your fault, but could not expect you to make any useful comment, rather as if, with Windscale about to go up and take England with it, you were to say, quickly, what is nuclear physics? It is too late. *(Pause.)*

JANE. Why did we stop talking? When was it? Do you remember?

COOPER. Jardine is a Communist.

JANE. If we went back —

COOPER. Communist on opium.

JANE. Please, shall we just —

COOPER. Opium of hatred! *(Pause.)*

JANE. Yes. All right.

COOPER. Listen. The man loathes himself.

JANE. Yes.

COOPER. Nothing worse. Nothing more likely to burst and scatter pain about. Never trust a man who hates himself.

JANE. I understand that.

COOPER. **I know these things.**

JANE. Yes.

COOPER.   Oh, God, the futility of this —

JANE *(standing, furiously).*   **I have stuck by you!** Through all your
   shudderings. Through all your blanknesses and sheer arctic silences. I
   have gone dry because of you. And I do not even think that it was love.
   Maybe it was honour. I only know I have had no nourishment from you.
   (Pause. COOPER stares at her.)

COOPER.   Jardine is here. How can I listen to you? I love you, but
   Jardine's here!

*He hurries out. JANE collapses back into her armchair. Her hand goes to her
crotch. Slowly, in the fade, she masturbates.*

Scene Two

*The moors, on a sunny day. BLOON and DOCKERILL appear, carrying a
picnic hamper and a rug. They stop, and shielding their eyes, stare back.*

BLOON.   It is a peculiar fact about this moor —

DOCKERILL.   Yes, isn't it?

BLOON.   You know what I'm going to say?

DOCKERILL.   Yes.

BLOON/DOCKERILL.   **Familiartiy breeds telepathy.**

BLOON.   We have walked for one-and-a-half hours and I feel I could
   reach out and touch it.

DOCKERILL.   We could always sit with our backs to it.

BLOON.   The sun is shining from the west, however. *(He sits, leans back.*
   DOCKERILL *remains standing, peering round. Pause.)*

DOCKERILL.   A Tizer bottle, abandoned by an environment-oblivious
   picnic party, has suffered fracture at the hoof of a moorland pony . . .
   (Pause.)

BLOON *(eyes closed in thought).*   The sun, now in its summer solstice,
   strikes the concave fragment at the potent angle of forty-five degrees,
   effecting magnification of — I hazard — not knowing the mica content of
   Tizer glass — one-hundred-and-fifty, and creates ignition on a bleached
   out packet of No. 6. The flame makes contact with the desiccated
   heather. There is a fifteen mile per hour wind. *(Pause.* DOCKERILL
   sits, lies back.) A minibus, containing twenty-two arthritic pensioners,
   had wandered off the official moorland road — *(giggling)* Aaaggghhhhh!

DOCKERILL.   All are asleep, in various garish, nylon-covered alloy
   chairs.

BLOON.   Aaaggghhhhh!

DOCKERILL *(warming to the subject).*   The familiar odour of smoulder-ing, piss-sodden hosiery — *(They are both falling into hysterics.)*

BLOON.   The sta- staccato bursts of exploding thermos flasks —

DOCKERILL.   Shooting their corks like champagne —

BLOON.   National Health wigs spontaneously del- del-

DOCKERILL.   **Deliquesce!**

BLOON.   Buckling walking frames —

To deep whoops of paralyzing laughter, they roll on the rug, unaware of COOPER, who has come up behind them with a shotgun and watches them with contempt. It dawns on them they are being watched. Pause.

COOPER.   Oh, you bastards. Oh, you loathsome servants of the opium fiend.

DOCKERILL.   Sorry?

COOPER.   Lying like lovers. Pink where your joints have rubbed. Hot-haired, giggling, nympho boys.

DOCKERILL *(sitting up).*   Watch it, mush.

COOPER.   Get off my moor. You wilt the precious flowers.

DOCKERILL.   I think you'll find this is a National Park. *(Pause. COOPER is staring at them.)*

BLOON *(of the gun).*   Please, would you point that somewhere else? Please?

DOCKERILL.   You're making my friend nervous.

Suddenly COOPER raises the gun to his shoulder, aiming it at BLOON, who lets out a whimper and rolls over onto his front.

DOCKERILL.   Oh, God. Oh, God.

COOPER.   His urine is so very eager. It sparkles in his groin . . .

DOCKERILL.   This is unforgivable.

COOPER.   You men of science, writing on your stiff white paper your mystical reports. You are the dirty men, you are the forensic filth. Jardine has your twin brains dancing on his finger-tips.

DOCKERILL.   I'm sorry, but I thought you might have wanted to dis-cover who burned your gaol. Obviously not.

COOPER.   Get off my moor. *(Pause. DOCKERILL looks at BLOON.)*

DOCKERILL.   Shall we?

BLOON.   Yes.

DOCKERILL.   All right. *(He bends to pick up the picnic basket.)*

COOPER.   Leave that.

DOCKERILL.   It's our basket.

COOPER.   You may not luxuriate. When I look around me it is the faceless experts who luxuriate, the men who have put their consciences to sleep. Go without your chicken legs for once.

DOCKERILL.   Well, perhaps we could just take the basket —

COOPER.   **Christ, don't gamble with a maiming, idiot!**

The inspectors run off. COOPER *watches them, then opens the basket. He removes a chicken leg and savages it. After a few moments, the sound of borzois is heard. He tosses away the remains.* TURK *bounds in, athletically.*

TURK.   Two fellars — one with wet trousers — Sheba would have a snap at it.

COOPER.   I have robbed them of their basket. Gorge yourself.

TURK.   I may do.

COOPER.   I was all shuddering you wouldn't be here.

TURK.   Oh, I'll come. What's this? *(He holds up a jar.)*

COOPER.   Turbot roe in aspic.

TURK.   What's turbot? What's aspic?

COOPER.   Don't play the illiterate, I am randy for a conversation. Mrs Cooper urged me to repair the whispering gallery of our marriage. It only reminded me how desperately I needed you.

TURK.   Here I am, then. *(He spoons the roe into his mouth.)*

COOPER.   Talk to me, Turk. I have been slashed about by Jardine, I am not my own master here.

TURK *(tossing the jar away).*   Shit. Like all upper-class grub it only tastes good because it's flavoured with a wallet.

COOPER.   Will you stop eating?

TURK.   I hear on the grapevine the Middenhurst blaze has made the bucket-shitters difficult. I hear they walk with their heads up for a few weeks. They are desperate to know who did it, to carry his picture on their shirts like Chairman Mao.

COOPER.   Middenhurst could have been an island in paradise. It could have swum in vegetation. What I offered them, instead of violence!

TURK.   Ivy round the locks. Rubber plants in solitary.

COOPER.   You are in a silly mood. When I need you so much. Unfortunate.

TURK.   You are wrung out, Cooper.

COOPER. Yes. So drop the mockery.

TURK *(taking an avocado from the basket).* What's this?

COOPER. **Do not pretend you do not know an avocado, liar!**

TURK. A proper basket, this is. *(Pause.)* I burned down Middenhurst. It's to my credit. *(Pause.)*

COOPER. Silly. **Why are you so fucking silly!**

TURK *(standing).* Rhodesia has got strictures in his rectum. He whimpers during evacuation. **Here, boy!**

COOPER. Turk, I plead with you.

TURK. It's all out now. Why don't you listen?

COOPER. You did it. I see. You must have your way.

TURK. With half-a-dozen tins of lacquer. In the broom cupboard. On No. 7 landing. With a cowgum fuse delayed by hessian. I am their hero, Cooper. I am the picture on the bucket-shitters' shirts.

COOPER. I suppose there is some need for you to entertain this fantasy. I suppose there is some absurd psychology in this.

TURK. There was a need all right, you smooth and slippery man.

COOPER. **I know what you have said has no truth in it.** All right? I know. Now talk to me before I weep.

TURK. There is no truth in me. I am Joe Turk.

COOPER. We have been so close, don't chuck it away.

TURK *(his Yorkshire dialect).* Time t'git dogs 'ome for missus.

COOPER. Turk, mercy on me.

TURK *(calling).* **Cum on thou tarty animal! Shakes rump like women's arses!**

COOPER *(with the gun).* **Turk, I have it in me to murder you!** *(TURK freezes. Pause.)* I brought you culture, you vile thing from the bush. And this is your reward to me. Hurry home. I have a terrible hurt and it makes me dangerous. *(Pause, then TURK runs off, athletically, whistling for the brozois. Pause.)* If I had died in Cyprus, bleeding in dusty Larnaca to the sound of running footsteps and the fumbling panic of café Greeks, I could not have done less with the stub of my life. I should have had a tablet in a church somewhere. Not rot like this.

Pause. Blackout.

Scene Three

C Hall: There are more papers on the desks. TURK *is sitting upright in the witness chair.* MATHESON *is alone, writing.* ANGELA *sits at her place. Pause. On two chairs opposite* ANGELA, *sit* BLOON *and* DOCKERILL.

TURK.   Do ya like me? I am a prince, a'n't A?

MATHESON.   Just sit quietly. *(Pause.)*

TURK.   A'm proud, a'n't A? Women juice for a proud man. *(*BLOON *coughs, uncomfortably.)*

MATHESON.   You are not allowed to talk to me.

TURK.   They all wet for a hero. *(He turns to* ANGELA.*)* A'n't that so, darlin'?

MATHESON.   Listen. It is contempt for you to chat to me in this way. You will wait until you're spoken to. Do you follow?

TURK.   But am A handsome? For all ma seven year. Am A not trim as a bluddy footballer?

MATHESON.   I will report this.

TURK.   Be honest, will ya? Am A not?

MATHESON.   Look, this will cost you —

TURK.   For what A am about to receive this will make no bluddy difference! If A were to cum clambering onto ya it cud na add a year to it! *(Pause.)*

MATHESON.   I ask because you see we have dispensed with police here and it creates a better atmosphere. If you sabotage it, we will have to get them back again. It is simply nicer, isn't it?

TURK.   Oh, Christ. It is nicer. Oh, Christ.

JARDINE *enters, patting his fly.*

JARDINE.   It is astonishing what a piss you can accumulate. I could have shattered glass with it. *(He sits at his desk.)*

MATHESON.   7787 Turk has been abusing me.

JARDINE.   Have you, mister? *(Pause.* TURK *just looks as* JARDINE *finds some papers. He looks up.)* I ask a question. *(Pause.)* You are like a python in the reptile house. *(Pause.)*

TURK.   I've come to tell.

JARDINE.   Yes, well, ye're a grass, are ye not? It is your habit.

TURK.   Will you take my words down? *(He looks to* ANGELA.*)*

JARDINE.   Are they treasures, then?

TURK. Your mission ends with me, Jardine.

JARDINE. What makes you so conclusive, then?

TURK. Are my words to be published? I need to know that or I don't speak.

JARDINE. Your vain literary ambition, is it? To be in a dusty ministry cellar?

TURK. You take me for a turd. I will show you I am not one. I ask for all my fellow sufferers in the archipelago.

JARDINE. Ah, he reads Solzhenitsyn. An educated thug, this one.

TURK. There were no books we could not get here. Education was on the agenda. As for being a thug, I resent that. Leave it out or I don't speak.

JARDINE. My papers tell me a postman is half-crazy following what you did to him. They had to wire his jaw and feed him through a nostril. I shudder.

TURK. It is not the matter here, is it!

JARDINE. No. But I am against your pride. There is an idea got around that criminals are rebels. They are not rebels, they are the lowest form of speculator, but instead of wielding money they wield — what was your currency — a hammer?

TURK (standing). I do not speak.

JARDINE. Oh, sit down. Ye've got by without pride long enough. (Pause.) Ye have an urge to shoot. Why don't ye? (Pause. Then TURK stands up, launches himself.)

TURK. The British Empire is not dead. Its sun will never set as long as there are prisons. The red coat, and the khaki, may have masqueraded as — (He dries, looks around to ANGELA.) I will start again, if that's all right. (Pause.) The British Empire is not dead. Its sun will never set as long as there are prisons. Shamed out of their effrontery, the red coat and the bloody khaki — (He stops, looks at JARDINE, who has got up and walked, hands behind his back, round the room.) Your walking about is throwing me . . . (JARDINE stops.) I am not fucking Aristotle. I can't talk on the trot.

JARDINE. Have you thought of speaking off the cuff? There is very little passion in a learned speech.

TURK. If you would not sabotage me, I could finish it! (JARDINE goes back to his chair.) Thank you. (Pause.) Where there is governing there is degradation. **Fact.** There can be no decent prison no matter how many carpets there may be, however many fucks you are permitted. I say that to all pipe-smoking lords and their obsession with conjugal visits. The club says everything. Without the club there is no prison. **Fact.** Ask any Indian what he remembers of the British. He will not say the architectural wonders of New Delhi. He will say the Scottish accent of a khaki corporal, the audacious jangling of his regimental belt, the sarcastic boots on gravel. They wear serge in this colony, to keep their kidneys warm, and double vests against the damp. Their shoes are rubber, under felt, to let them creep up to our spy holes undetected. A riot, and they break our heads. So far, so good. A colony is a colony no matter what the climate. Be grateful to the man who clubs you, for he keeps you sane. *(Pause.)* Come Cooper, though, comes creeping death, Lord Douglas-Home style, white and subtle, hung his rifle up behind the door, sees only nastiness in the old type governor, thick and bent, and has angelic leanings, wants to make the natives human and wear suits, chats to rapists like his pretty nephews home on vac, and is **most fucking dangerous,** growing nasturtiums up against the granite. *(Pause.)* But all his hand-shaking, lending out his first editons to illiterates, all his first-name democratic stickiness, put proper terror in the screws, panicked our special sadist Mr Whip, and even brought old Udy to indulge his fists. On the one hand, there was this glad-handed Tory saint, and on the other, spitting gaolers feeling the flagstones shift beneath their feet. It was a painful tension for the inmates, to phrase it in a whisper. *(Pause.)* I burned down the gaol, Mr Jardine. Tell 'em in Whitehall there is no reconciling E.M. Forster with a kicking in the testicles. *(Pause.)*

JARDINE.   You have buckets of eloquence, Turk. Do you have prison facilities to thank for that?

TURK.   I was Cooper's darling grass. I was his peach. All the greatest authors came my way, with best wishes on the fly-leaf. It rubs off. Also I am, in my way, a genius.

JARDINE.   What way is that?

TURK.   In all this prison, only Cooper knew I was intelligent.

JARDINE.   Why the seven-year performance, then?

TURK.   Long sentences bring men to slobber. It is very helpful if you need to concentrate, on no matter what futility. Anyway, I was content enough with Cooper's company. We commiserated on the obduracy of the criminal intelligence.

JARDINE.   He opened his heart to you?

TURK.   He did that. It was a kind of blue colour. *(Pause.)*

JARDINE.   Miss Matheson will question you.

MATHESON.   Are you a hero, Mr Turk?

TURK.   Yes. But I rely on you to spread my gospel. Through the Stationery Office, for the full text. The Daily Mirror for the rest.

MATHESON.   You would like to see all prisons burned to the ground?

TURK.   Why stint ourselves? Prisons are the start of it.

MATHESON. England?

TURK. Fire spreads.

MATHESON. That's rather a commonplace remark for you.

TURK. Liberty is catching. How's that?

MATHESON. And yet in the last five minutes you have effectively deprived yourself of it. I see you were due to be paroled in seven weeks.

TURK. Madam, liberty is the product of action. It is not walking about sniffing the street. There are millions walking the streets in what you glibly describe as liberty who have not the faintest notion what it is, nor would they miss it if you ripped it from them. I am more at liberty from what I did than the whole County of Surrey. Or the work force of British Leyland, for that matter.

MATHESON. Perhaps you would not thrive outside of prison.

TURK. It is a university for those who want to use it. And I don't mean the way the stupid con suggests. Safe-blowing is for idiots when you can read your country in a gaoler's look.

JARDINE. Well, I am deeply moved by your politics. How is your fire-raising?

TURK. Meaning what?

JARDINE. How did ye do it?

TURK. Why ask me? It's in the report. I did not rub two sticks together. I assure you of that.

JARDINE. In your own words, though. You read so much better than the colourless English these gentlemen have culled together. *(Pause.)*

TURK. There is a broom cupboard on No. 7 landing. It used to be up there somewhere. *(He glances up.)* Six tins of lacquer, used for re-surfacing the bunks, burn very brightly. Explode in fact. Being a half-wit, and therefore trusted, I was allowed access at times when the rest were not. My fuse burned very slowly. I had worked on it a year at least. Perhaps if you don't know already, I had better keep that to myself. There are other fires to consider. *(Long pause. JARDINE just looks at him.)* You look at me like I ought to be murdered, Stannheim manner.

JARDINE. I do not. It is pity. It gives me no pleasure to tell you your status as a hero comes to grief in this room. *(Pause. TURK glares at him.)*

TURK. You are suppressing it.

JARDINE. I suppress nothing.

TURK. It will get out. There were riots long before newspapers. We have communication. It is called the human voice.

JARDINE. I suppress nothing.

TURK.   In a gaol the colour of the governor's pants is common knowledge. Do you think some Secrets Act will stifle —

JARDINE.   **Ye do not listen, do ye!**

TURK.   **I do not!** Seven years I have been listening. I tell you the borzois'
barking was music compared to anything human that came out of here!

JARDINE.   Well, try me, mister. I give it to you straight. Whoever
burned the prison down, it was not you. *(Pause.)*

TURK.   Liar. *(Pause.)* **Dirt-encrusted liar.**

JARDINE.   I tolerate the language, but it's wasted. The people you
should be cursing are sitting mouse-like over there. It is their facts that
stagger you. *(He picks up a fire report, drops it again.)* They will have it
your fire came and went.

TURK.   **Lacquer! Lacquer in the broom cupboard!**

JARDINE.   They have a dozen reasons why the real thing started somewhere else. *(He looks at them.)* Would you gentlemen elaborate? I don't
have your expertise.

BLOON/DOCKERILL *(rising together)*.   From our investigation —

JARDINE.   It carries no more conviction to be doubled. If truth were
related to unanimity, Nuremburg would be a shrine, wouldn't it? And
boy scouts' dib, dib, dibbing, a collective oracle. One will do. *(BLOON
sits.)*

DOCKERILL.   From our investigation it was evident that a secondary
source of fire had been initiated on the second floor of the main building
in the room described as Broom Cupboard, No. 86A on the plan —
(BLOON stands, shakes out a map, and points.) This was ignited by a
fuse of compressed hessian and glue, probably cowgum with traces of
common candle-wax. The time of this small fire was estimated to be
about nine o'clock p.m. Six tins of Monohydrate Dioloxin-based paint
lacquer ignited. The remains of these tins were examined. They are
numbered C20 to C26 in the index of exhibits, Appendix VII, Latin
numerals. *(BLOON indicates the back pages of the report.)* We are
confident this fire did not spread beyond the immediate region of its
source for the following reasons. Flame scalding on the back wall of the
cupboard indicates a spread of only ninety centimetres or less. The
close-fitting nature of the door, and the fact that it was locked, prevented
the inflow of sufficient oxygen to enhance the rapid rise in temperature
consistent with chemical-based flame. Whilst the cupboard was severely
damaged, the direction of the fire was from beneath, via the second-floor
joists, the course of which is positively established in Section II, Latin
numerals. *(He sits. Pause.)*

TURK.   There is no depth of prostitution to which you bland creatures
would not sink. You have pissed on science, which the poor and ignorant
regard as piss-proof. It is not. Your sick bladder drips. *(Pause. BLOON
coughs.)*

DOCKERILL *(to* JARDINE*).* Are we allowed to come back on this?

TURK. **Come back on it! Lie doctors!** If expediency required it, the world would go back to being flat!

DOCKERILL. We are doing a job, the criteria for which are entirely objective —

TURK. Flannel me some more. Flannel me. You are **political things.** Get back to your bungalows, and giggle over your tea.

DOCKERILL. I am sorry, but this is not the first time —

JARDINE. No thank you, Mr Dockerill.

DOCKERILL. I would like the right to —

JARDINE. You would like, but time forbids it. Angela has noted your protest. *(*DOCKERILL *sits.* JARDINE *looks to* TURK.*)* The fire that did the damage had its origin in a smart lady's woolly. You are not partial to lady's woollies, are ye, Turk?

TURK. I don't speak seriously to what is a snigger shared by all of you. I am not mocked.

JARDINE. I appreciate your cynicism. I reek with it myself. But the report has not been tampered with. I give my word. *(*TURK *gets up.)*

TURK. I will not waste my breath on a dishonest man.

JARDINE. I resent that.

TURK. And I jeer at your resentment. *(He starts to go out.)*

JARDINE. You have forfeited my pity for that.

TURK. **His pity! He takes back his pity! Oh, his pity, I am going to miss that!**

JARDINE. You have a great hurt. I am sorry I am the one that gave it you.

TURK. **I am not hurt.**

Pause. He stares at JARDINE *for a long time, then suddenly, sweeping up the chair, he brings it crashing down on the stone floor. Methodically, he reduces it to sticks, then goes out. Pause.*

ANGELA. Blimey. I thought he was gonna hit somebody with it. *(She giggles.)*

JARDINE. Stupid. A proper stupid. Mr Dockerill, would you complete the metaphor and replace the chair? *(*DOCKERILL *goes out.* BLOON *folds up the reports and goes out after him.)*

MATHESON. You sympathized.

JARDINE. Sympathize? Christ, woman, there is too much pain in the world for the indulging of gestures. I would have him burning gaols better than maiming postmen all the same. He is a graduate from a certain kind of filth.

DOCKERILL *(entering with a chair).* It's not quite the same as the other —

JARDINE. Nor will the new gaol look like the old one. But it is a chair. That is its significance. *(DOCKERILL puts it down, goes out.)*

MATHESON. Human nature won't just endure, will it? Thank God. Eventually, it chucks a brick. I am very glad of that. I am glad of human dignity.

JARDINE. Observe the new chair. I say no more on that one. There is a new chair.

MATHESON. Yes, but —

JARDINE. Let us have change. But change that matters. Is there anything on Ponting yet?

MATHESON. They are dragging all the little ponds. The Black Pool had one dead pony in it.

JARDINE. Ponting would not jump in a pond.

MATHESON. They found his tie beside it.

JARDINE. Ponting is drinking tea with his mother. With an open-necked shirt.

MATHESON. Not according to his mother.

JARDINE. Mothers are incorrigible liars.

MATHESON. Can't you accept that Barry had a crisis?

JARDINE. Barry had a crisis? **Barry had a crisis?** Sounds like he started menstruating. The only crisis he had was constipation. *(Suddenly,* COOPER *bursts in.)*

COOPER. **You sent for me, did you not?**

JARDINE. Yes.

COOPER. **Then do not keep me waiting. That is common decency. That is manners. Is there any manners here?**

JARDINE. We do our best, Colonel. But our specialist in manners disappeared. Some have it in a pond, but I say to Guildford. Please take a seat.

COOPER. You and your please. Teeth and hypocrisy.

JARDINE. Just sit down, then. You are a big man and you wave your arms about. You will frighten our young lady. *(COOPER doesn't move.)* Why don't ye sit!

COOPER. In Malaya we interrogated terrorists in chairs. We made a mockery of hospitality. *(Pause.)*

JARDINE.   Christ, you are deathly tired, Cooper. Like a prime minister with a secret bleeding . . . *(Pause.)*

COOPER.   I am a good man.

JARDINE.   Is that so?

COOPER.   Very good. Please treat me appropriately.

JARDINE.   Alas, if I took men at their own valuation, the young girl's notebook would be bland indeed.

COOPER.   You are a Communist.

JARDINE.   In the Queen's service? What is England coming to?

COOPER.   You have a longing to do violence. I see the look. I found it in the eyes of snapping terrorists. I've seen it in the bucket-shitter. No man ever took more loathing on himself than me. You are the vermin that sprang from Lenin's shit.

JARDINE.   Shall we swop chairs, Cooper? You are interrogating me.

COOPER.   Oh, why don't you come clean? Have you no honour? God, our poor country will squirm under your breed.

JARDINE.   Cooper, you have poked out your Sandhurst lower lip at a whole globeful of foreigners, and now you dare to thrust it out at me. I am not to be abused. This is my inquiry. I order you. Be ordered and bugger you. *(He looks to* ANGELA.*)* Strike out the last phrase, bugger you.

COOPER.   I forgive you.

JARDINE.   You forgive me.

MATHESON.   I wonder if we wouldn't do better to pursue a line of questioning? Carry on from where we stopped?

JARDINE.   It would be better. It would be music to Angela's tattered ears.

MATHESON.   Colonel Cooper, on your first day as Governor here you delivered an address to the assembled officers on the theme of Holiness. What impression do you think that made?

COOPER.   They decided I was cracked.

MATHESON.   What did you mean by Holiness?

COOPER.   I meant the beauty of good government.

MATHESON.   Beauty?

COOPER.   Yes. There is none higher.

JARDINE.   Rather puzzling this concept, to a simple British screw?

COOPER.   I was out to build Paradise. Ordinary brick-laying would not do. Yet I had ordinary brickies.

JARDINE.   Just so.

MATHESON.   How exactly was Middenhurst to be transformed? Considering there were three men to a cell, and their slops to keep them company?

COOPER.   If you think Paradise is a flushing lavatory, you are unlikely to arrive there.

MATHESON.   At the risk of appearing shallow, I must say I think sanitation matters.

COOPER.   It is a different sort of perfection I refer to. Materialists are glued to futile innovation and sensual greed.

JARDINE.   For a man with two hundred bottles of Château Lafite in his cellar, that comes very unconvincing, Cooper.

COOPER.   You value everything. You are obsessed with price and width.

JARDINE.   No. I have a nose for hypocrites. I am a right Pinocchio for that.

MATHESON.   I wonder if I might carry on?

JARDINE.   Carry on, yes. I am sorry for my interruption, but something was twisting my bollocks. *(Pause.)* All right, I have uncrossed my legs. *(Pause.)*

MATHESON.   The Holy sort of governing, could you elaborate?

COOPER.   There is a way of governing the human animal. It is to club him, to concuss his head. By bruising and rupturing, to fog it with persistent aches. There is two thousand years of history in that, of useless whimpering in African groves and frosty German villages. But deep inside the bloody head flickers the feeble light of service, the will to joyfully obey. It burned in our first ancestor and it does now in every raping Kurd and flaming Irishman. I wanted to blow on that feeble light until it burned strong and pure as a gas, to feed it with culture until every snarling, blaspheming thing that launched its head against our bars and made the cell floor run with its saliva, rose to the silence of its dignity! *(Pause.)*

MATHESON.   And did they? *(Pause.)*

COOPER.   No. They resisted me. You give your heart, and they examine it, and pass it round, nudging and giggling like niggers round a white man's skin.

JARDINE.   Did you hate them very much?

COOPER.   Must not. Must not hate them.

JARDINE.   Of course not. Not becoming in a saint. Resent them, then?

COOPER. Tried not to.

JARDINE. Yes, but all the same —

COOPER. **Tried. Tried, obviously.**

JARDINE. But in the end, got the better of you. Only human, after all . . .

COOPER. Yelling, every face showing the red back of its throat, pressing the policemen's backs, and stinking, had to hold my book up, my *Howard's End*, to keep their saliva off my wife, and the Commissioner kept saying, may we shoot over their heads? Shoot! Shoot! All he could think of. Yes, I said, shoot! Shoot!

JARDINE. Didn't love you, did they? After all you'd sacrificed? *(Pause.)*

COOPER. She had a carrier-bag of old clothes for the jumble sale. *(Pause.)*

JARDINE. Ah. *(Pause.)*

COOPER. While they were in their slumber, often used to walk the landings, in felt slippers, with my screw. In dead of night, to hear their gurgling. English sleep so noisy, so much flinging of the arms and legs. Not like Malays. Little birds in nests, who never moved. *(Pause.)*

JARDINE. The old clothes, you said. *(Pause.)* Cooper. *(Pause.)*

COOPER. Some cardigans she never wore. I took them with me to — *(He stops, seeing, from his chair,* JANE *come into the hall. She is bleeding profusely from the head.)*

JARDINE. Don't stop *(Pause.)* **Don't stop!**

JANE. Something has gone wrong with Turk.

They turn. ANGELA *lets out a little scream.* MATHESON *rises to her feet.*

JARDINE. Oh, Cooper, what anger they had bottled up for you!

ANGELA. I'm going to faint.

JARDINE. Don't faint! Not now! You mustn't faint!

COOPER. Is that my wife?

JARDINE. Cooper, did you try to burn them in their beds?

ANGELA *(fainting).* I'm sorry — I can't stand — blood —

JARDINE. **Sod it, Angela! Do not faint! I order you!** *(She collapses.)* Fuck. That ends the session, I suppose. *(Pause.)*

JANE. I asked him, would he care to trim the beech hedge, and he did this to me . . .

Blackout.

Scene Four

*The moors. In the blackout, the sound of a shotgun being fired, first one
barrel, then the other. Lights up on* STAGG *gazing along the barrel. Nearby,*
JARDINE, *with flask to his lips, Pause.*

STAGG.   Not supposed to shoot at kestrels, are yer? That thing hanging
up there, hovering like. *(Pause.)* Christ, though, it does keep still! *(He
lowers the gun and stuffs a cartridge in the breech.)* Can't go back
empty-handed, can I? They will take me for a banana. *(He aims.)* Bugger
me, it's dived into the heather.

JARDINE.   Home Secretary, I'm following ye about like a fucking gun-
dog and the result is I am getting drunk. I cannot get enthusiastic about
knocking birds down, even for the sake of Socialism.

STAGG.   I detect the mockery, Jardine, but I would make the point, the
best things in life are not free, pop songs to the contrary notwithstanding.
(Gazing for a target.) Dogs, horses, shooting. We shall have 'em in our
turn. Having wiped away the snot of snobbery, of course. I read that
Durham miners have started polo. On bicycles, of course, but it's a
beginning. Can you see a bloody bird?

JARDINE.   You have frightened 'em away. Shooting is like politics, it is a
stealthy business.

STAGG.   I'm very glad we managed to be on our own.

JARDINE.   Ye did no have to bring me up here for that privilege.

STAGG.   Possibly. But you get very cautious when you're holding office.
The glorious free press and so on. I don't think even Chapman Pincher
has bugged the moors. I am asking you a favour.

JARDINE.   I don't do favours.

STAGG.   Did I say a favour? I meant, will you take a bribe?

JARDINE.   I don't need money. I have spent too long with men who
sucked on it.

STAGG.   Quite. It wasn't money I was offering. *(Pause.)* Do you want a
suit of armour, George?

JARDINE.   A what?

STAGG.   Oh, come on, do you wanna be a knight? We are fetching up the
Honours List. *(Pause.)*

JARDINE.   That's no favour. I am entitled to it. (STAGG *shrugs.)* Old
boy, it would be a stinking outrage if I were overlooked. I have given my
life to this rotting Commonwealth!

STAGG.   Well, yes, but we are looking into titles. We are going to make
do with less.

JARDINE.   Christ, the party is in earnest with its cuts!

STAGG.   I hope you aren't going to indulge in loony leftist leanings, George. My ears are getting clogged with it.

JARDINE.   **Do I get my title, Jesus Christ!**

STAGG.   I had no idea you felt so strongly.

JARDINE.   I feel strongly about the boss-class, but I would not have a man refuse his wages.

STAGG.   Excellent. I'm glad to hear it.

JARDINE.   I am an old man and I won't be overlooked!

STAGG.   We hope not, George. Which brings me to the other matter, doesn't it? *(Pause.)* Cooper mustn't take no stick. *(Pause.)* Christ, there's that bloody kestrel or whatever. Can't it see I've got a gun, daft git? *(He lifts the gun, aims it, holds the posture for some seconds, then lowers the gun.)* I don't kill kestrels, George. They are England's heritage. *(He lays the gun on the ground.)* I don't care who takes the credit, but Cooper is no arsonist. Official.

JARDINE.   You are asking me to doctor it.

STAGG.   You comprehend me to the hilt.

JARDINE.   In forty years no one has asked me that before.

STAGG.   You have been lucky. *(Pause.)* The other geezer, Turk. He wants the glory. Let him carry it. *(Pause.)*

JARDINE.   Christ, have you no honour? *(Pause. STAGG looks at him, pityingly.)*

STAGG.   Oh, dear, we are digging up the corpse of political morality. The point of the inquiry, George, is to make sure the cause of its inception does not recur. It is not to jab a finger at somebody, is it? Or throw rotten eggs? Cooper is a sick man. We see no point in crucifying him.

JARDINE.   I do.

STAGG.   Yes, well, you're a crucifixion addict, aren't you?

JARDINE.   Stagg, in a society like this, which you have stroked and fondled for so long, there is so little justice it is a crime to temper it with mercy. When you have fixed the justice, I will show the mercy.

STAGG.   Really, George, you are so basic. You are a bit of a turnip, aren't you? And I'm asparagus in cream.

JARDINE.   Do not George me, please. The familiarity is sticking in my nose. As for being a turnip, you appointed me to find the arsonist. I have done so. Now the public has its rights, and no fucking poncey vegetable can stop it.

STAGG.   It is the dear old public I am thinking of.

JARDINE.   **Well, let 'em hear!**

STAGG.   You do shout. You do get violent. *(He looks round.)* Chapman Pincher wouldn't need a mike to pick us up.

JARDINE.   The crime. The truth. The punishment.

STAGG.   Very fundamental. Like this gaol. Scotch granite. When we live in a world which is so very subtle. I must tell you, Jardine, and I'm sorry you won't let me call you George, because I have a sneaking admiration for your type, a sextant is no use to a coal-miner. *(Pause. JARDINE looks confused.)* I mean a moral code is all very well but sometimes you have to scrub it! There's an election coming up **and that's a cabinet secret, all right, Mr Pincher?** *(He utters this loud with his hands to his mouth.)* Governors setting light to prisons isn't very good for confidence. It so happens I appointed him myself. *(He reaches for* JARDINE'S *flask.)* Give us a swig of that, will yer? (JARDINE *doesn't relinquish it.)* Oh, blimey, you are petty, George! *(Pause.)*

JARDINE.   I was a Major in the war.

STAGG.   Were you? I missed it.

JARDINE.   I had a bren-gun section, thirty miles outside Dunkirk. On one end of a bridge they had forgotten to blow up.

STAGG.   Hello, hello. Frank Sinatra.

JARDINE.   We were the rear guard. We had to stop the Germans crossing it. It was a hot day. Out of the heat haze came six figures, slowly, onto the bridge. Six nuns. I said to my corporal, tell the fucking nuns to stop. So he stood up and waved at them, and they waved back, giggling like Audrey fucking Hepburn. So I said, fire over their heads. They stopped, and then came on again, making signs of crosses and what not. And I said, all right, kill them, but my gunner refused the order. I argued that the Germans often dressed as nuns, it was a well-known fact, but still he wouldn't, so I arrested him and took his place, by which time these nuns were chanting and holding out their crosses to us and it was very obvious that they were women, any bugger could see that. But I was in the grip of longing, I could not hold myself. Professional virgins who trusted the superstition of their habit to excuse them anything. I fired, and I loved firing, even at that disgusting range. *(Pause.)* And now you come to me, chanting the Red Flag, and trusting in the superstition of your parliamentary habit . . . *(Pause. He shakes his head.)* My finger's still on the trigger. Ye shall not pass. *(Pause.)*

STAGG.   You can hate me if you want, George. Lots of people do. Snobs and swindlers staggering round night spots, squires and gangsters swigging *blanc de blancs* in pastel-coloured Range Rovers. I expect they'd welcome you.

JARDINE.   That's cheap. Ye know it is.

STAGG.   All right.

JARDINE.   **That's cheap!** *(Pause.)*

STAGG.   George, we happen to be lumbered here with what they call the party-system, the Westminster model, call it what you like. And the bulk of the population of this long-suffering island of ours are under the impression it is freedom. The thought of this freedom no doubt gives comfort to old ladies dying of neglect in tower-blocks. It is no doubt shouted from the terraces by fifteen year-old illiterates. But it is what we've got and we 'ave got to work with it, bent and crippled as it is. Nothing is perfect, least of all corruption, but the smelly old women and the schizophrenic kids don't give a bugger for your morals. We did not choose the system, but **we have got to get the hang of it.** *(Pause.)* I have not got clean hands, George. I am not pure. I will be laid to rest to all the jeers of history. But I serve. By Christ, **I serve.** *(Pause.)*

JARDINE.   You ask me to be guilty. I have never been guilty before.

STAGG.   Guilty, George? Guilty before whom?

JARDINE.   **Before me.** *(Pause.)*

STAGG.   Quite. There comes a time you 'ave to stop polishing yer conscience. Yer end up hypnotized by it.

JARDINE.   If there were anything left — you — or anything — worthy of my sacrifice, I would not hesitate. But there is nothing. Ye are all dirty and discredited.

STAGG.   Poor George. The world 'as let him down. The 'uman race has failed him . . . *(Pause.)* George . . . ye 'ave to cling, ol' son. No matter how often men fall, how often they betray yer . . . **Cling** . . . there's nowt else . . . *(JARDINE looks at him, then turns to go.)* There's drinks at Mrs Cooper's. Answer me by then. *(Pause. STAGG picks up the shotgun, looks out for a target. Suddenly he lets out a cry.)* Oi! You! *(He beckons.)* Come on. Ain't gonna bite yer. *(PONTING comes in, as a green-man, in shreds of clothing. Round his waist a string of dead blackbirds.)* 'Ow much do yer want for the birds? *(PONTING just looks at him.)* A quid for the lot. *(Pause.)* All right, a fiver. *(He digs out his wallet.)* Here, look. Five birds. Five nicker. *(He points to the note.)* Big white Queen. 'Er picture, see? Promises to pay to the bearer, all right? Come on, you know what a —

PONTING.   I don't have any use for money, I'm afraid. *(Pause.)*

STAGG.   What is this? A rag stunt?

PONTING.   I live here.

STAGG.   What — here —

PONTING.   On the moor. *(Pause.)*

STAGG.   It's not allowed. There aren't no proper lavatories.

PONTING.   You can have the brids. I found them hanging on a fence. *(He undoes the string.)*

STAGG. Christ, they pong a bit.

PONTING. You get used to things being a little less than fresh.

STAGG *(taking them)*. A waste this, isn't it?

PONTING. I probably wouldn't have eaten them in any case.

STAGG. You, I mean. *(Pause.)* You have education. I can tell that at a glance.

PONTING. I am not fit.

STAGG. Fitter than I am. I couldn't last a night out here.

PONTING. Fit to live with people.

STAGG. Balls.

PONTING. I am power-crazy.

STAGG. What's wrong with that?

PONTING. I'm dangerous.

STAGG. Me too.

PONTING. Resist it, then.

STAGG. Like fuck I will. *(Pause.)* Oh, to be really dangerous, son. To be **thoroughly bloody dangerous.** To know your coming in a room has set the decanters shaking and the palsied hands of dowagers and flowery-shirted old tycoons fluttering on the damask. To know that Bad Men have the horrors of you, and though obliged to shake it, catch the terrors from your sweaty hand. *(Pause.)* Don't be afraid of being dangerous. That is a silly humanism. That is licking the rims of jolly hockey sticks okay. *(Pause.)* Ta for the oiseaux.

Blackout.

Scene Five

The COOPERS' *drawing room. A lifeless party is in progress.* COOPER *is alone in an armchair.* JANE, *wearing a head-scarf over her bandage, is standing with* MATHESON. BLOON *and* DOCKERILL *stand together by the window.* ANGELA *is alone, intent upon a cherry in her drink.*

BLOON. I love parties.

DOCKERILL. Meeting new people.

BLOON. Fun and dancing.

DOCKERILL. My name's Craig.

BLOON. Oh, that is lovely!

DOCKERILL.   Do you think so?

BLOON.   Oh, I love it.

DOCKERILL.   You look rather like a Carol.

BLOON.   Do I really?

DOCKERILL.   Don't ask me why.

BLOON.   I am a Carol.

BLOON/DOCKERILL.   **Oh, what a wonderful world!** *(They honk with laughter.)*

JANE.   It is a funny thing about us, isn't it? That we will take the best wine from our cellars and offer it to people who have abused us? One day he unlocked the gaol at Nicosia and saluted murderer after murderer as they came blinking out into the sun. You bear us no ill will, they said, monkey-grinning as foreigners do. That is a sign of a mature race. *(Enter, fairly drunk,* STAGG *and* JARDINE.*)*

STAGG.   We had a warm-up in the Stagg's Arms. They are naming bloody hotels after me. (JANE *offers him a glass from a tray.)*

JANE.   Not so much a hotel. More a doss-house, Mr Stagg.

STAGG.   Christ, what's this, Château-bottled, I assume?

JANE.   We are removing none to Knightsbridge, so make yourself free.

STAGG.   The way this woman talks. This particular la-di-da lady who on the backs of the worst-paid workers in the developed world, lays in crates of Château Lafite 1953. *(He drinks.)* Christ, it is good *(He gulps.)* Here's to a better world!

JANE *(to* JARDINE*).*   I imagine you will not be bothering Middenhurst again?

JARDINE.   Madam, wild horses would not drag my corpse within the precincts of this place. I am pissed, but not on the local brewery. Despair can make you stagger just as well.

STAGG *(moving across the room to* BLOON *and* DOCKERILL*).*   Good evening, lads. Now, which of you is Tweedle-Dum, it's slipped my mind. Would that be you? *(He looks at* BLOON.*)* You know what I think, I think you are Siamese and some quack has made the join invisible. Must be here somewhere — *(He chops the air between them with his hand.)* Nope. Nope. Damned clever thing, the National Health. Which one of you has got the cock? *(He turns back to* JANE.*)* I hope I am not befouling the air with my common diction, madam. No doubt a borzoi will have my throat out if I do. *(He walks unsteadily towards her.)* The borzoi, incidentally, was trained to bite peasants under the Czars. Did you know that, Jardine? The Reds were gonna eliminate the breed, but thought better of it. They adapted very well to sniffing out the Romanovs. Now there's a moral there. *(Pause.)* Christ, I love a party but

— *(He notices* ANGELA.*)* Drink up, darling, it's amazing what a decent glass of wine can do to knicker elastic. *(He looks up at the window.)* Now there's a view. Sunset on the moors. England as she lives and breathes. No bloody Arab shall have that off us, shall he? *(He steps further forward, breathes deep.)* Oh, roses, what a picture! Lady Jane, you have been busy with the secateurs. *(He closes his eyes, breathes deep again.)* It is an interesting fact that William Morris would have picked up, I've no doubt, that one of the most noxious inequalities of capitalism is in the distribution of the view. My grandad's bedroom window was two feet from a railway viaduct. 7 per cent of the population have got 84 per cent of the best views. *(He turns suddenly.)* **I am bloody serious!** *(He glares, then turns back to breathe.)*

JANE.   My husband hates your being here. He thinks the barbarians have got into the Citadel.

STAGG.   We have, Mrs, but when we look at all the treasures, we get mesmerized. When the Romans got back to their temples I expect they found half the Vandals whimpering on their knees. I am whimpering out loud, that's all. *(He looks over his shoulder.)* George, where does a bloke go for a slash round here?

JARDINE.   Where ye're standing, I imagine. Down the leg.

STAGG.   Join me, will yer? Piss for socialism. Piddle Martyrs we shall be. *(*JARDINE *goes to him, stands at his shoulder. They urinate.)* Well, son? What's it to be?

JANE.   He is urinating on my Harry Wheatcrofts . . .

JARDINE.   I am laying down my honour. For your honour.

STAGG.   Good. You are a hero of the English people. I mean that. Christ, all this piss! I haven't had so much fun since I hung a sheep's guts on the altar!

JARDINE.   Stagg, ye give the Coopers of this world too much bloody dignity. *(He starts to walk away.)*

STAGG.   Sorry, George. I am not in the aquiline-nosed-how-d'ye-do business. Let 'em win on etiquette. I will — *(He stops, shudders.)* **Oh, Jesus Christ** . . . *(Pause. Then he stumbles backwards.)* Is my cock in? *(He falls to the floor.* ANGELA, *horrified, drops her glass, which breaks.* JARDINE *turns back.)*

JARDINE.   Oh, there is some justice lingering. . . !

BLOON.   Man holding whisky glass experiences cardiac arrest at evening drinks.

DOCKERILL.   Releases tumbler, which shatters on impact with polyurethaned pine floor.

JANE.   The Minister has fallen off his pins. The Queen's Man, this is. Oh, my poor country! *(She looks to* COOPER.*)*

JARDINE *(who has gone to look at* STAGG*)*.   Ye're frothing at the gob, man. All the fixing, and the footling, and the flannel's pouring out of you! All the scum of yer lungs, the drivel of a useless life deserting you!

ANGELA.   Please stop, I think he's dying!

JARDINE *(unable to contain himself)*.   Where are yer smarting phrases now? Where is yer platform magic?

MATHESON *(cognizant of the situation, coming over)*.   Stop it.

JARDINE.   Bubbles on yer fat tongue! Put it in, Stagg, I do not wanna see it, **don't stick your great black tongue at me!**

MATHESON *(pulling him away)*.   **Stop it!** *(She stares at him in horror.)*

BLOON.   He has a little wife somewhere.

DOCKERILL.   Answers to the name of Aud.

BLOON.   No conversationalist, but very clean.

BLOON/DOCKERILL.   **After you with the mouthwash!**

They go to STAGG *and start a kiss-of-life resuscitation. At that moment,* PONTING *appears, dressed in a dark suit several sizes too large for him and clearly borrowed.*

PONTING.   Mr Jardine. I've come back to be dangerous.

Blackout.

Scene Six

C hall. It is dark, but for a shaft of moonlight from one of the high windows. After a few moments, MATHESON *comes in. She hesitates.*

MATHESON.   George? *(Pause.)* Oh, come on, George? *(Pause.)*

JARDINE.   Stand there. I want to look at ye.

MATHESON *(in the light)*.   All right?

JARDINE.   Not yet. *(Pause.)* Elizabeth, we shan't be sitting together any more.

MATHESON.   No.

JARDINE.   No more giggles on the Inter-City. No more adjoining bed-rooms in hotels.

MATHESON.   No. *(Pause.)* Sir George.

JARDINE.   I cannot face ye, but I want ye to listen. I have years ahead of me to suffer in consulting rooms, and long, dirty months of dying. The title will make them treat me better. It is human nature, but it is a fact . . . *(Pause.)*

MATHESON. I don't believe that is the reason.

JARDINE. Oh, do ye not?

MATHESON. No. *(Pause.)*

JARDINE. Elizabeth, have I not been an immaculate man? Have I not
been the perfect servant? Don't question me. I am going home to study
roses. *(Pause.)*

MATHESON. England brings you down at last . . .

There is a flash of torches. MATHESON *quickly moves into the shadows.*
WHIP *and* UDY *come in, uniformed in great coats. They quickly run their
lamps over the walls.*

UDY. Did you ever lay that turd?

WHIP. Eventually.

UDY. Did it help?

WHIP. It cured me.

UDY. Keep it to yerself, will you? Don't want everybody doing it. *(He
walks a little way.)* I thought Jardine a man somewhat fatigued. Not
cutting. I sensed some nibbling death. The grapevine said he was a
bugger, but I danced over him.

WHIP. They came, they saw, they whitewashed.

UDY. Cool all of a sudden. Now he's got his bags packed for Whitehall.

WHIP. Printed matter never bruised.

UDY. Full of wisdom. My own wisdom, but never mind. *(He shines his
torch high along the wall.)* To think blokes squatted up there, lost in
sordid little dreams. Two hundred years of it. Oh, History! Oh, England!
(They start walking out.)

WHIP *(as on a routine night).* **Orl present an' c'rrect, sah!**

UDY. **Goo' night, everyone!**

*They go out. Pause of some ten seconds, then the shaft of moonlight fades out
to a black.*

HEAVEN

CHARACTERS

OLD BEVIN
BEVIN
MRS BRAYBON
CHAUFFEUR
MOSCROP
KAREN
DIVER
STOAT
WARDER
SLAUGHTERFORD
SLESS
FIRST TOURIST
SECOND TOURIST
ST LEGER
ZENA

The Deceased

BRAYBON
ST LEGER THE ELDER
JONES
SMITH
BROWN
EDWARDS
DEAD BEVIN

Heaven was commissioned by BBC Television's 'Play of the Week' in 1978. It awaits a production.

Scene One

A churchyard in the country. Two labourers are sprawled under a tree, drinking tea from a flask.

OLD BEVIN.   Sir Dennis be dead, thun.

BEVIN.   Aye.

OLD BEVIN.   Of drinkin'.

BEVIN.   Aye.

OLD BEVIN.   An' drownin'.

BEVIN.   I hear so.

OLD BEVIN.   Killed all 'en peacocks.

BEVIN.   Aye.

OLD BEVIN.   T'was terrible.

BEVIN.   They tell me.

OLD BEVIN.   Brewed 'us own gin, see?

BEVIN.   They say so.

OLD BEVIN.   Berserked 'un.

BEVIN.   Would do so.

OLD BEVIN.   Wrote filth on 'us wall.

BEVIN.   Ol' bugger.

OLD BEVIN.   Then fell in the water.

BEVIN.   They tell me. *(Pause.)*

OLD BEVIN.   Shall 'ave caravans now, thun.

BEVIN.   Thank Jesus.

OLD BEVIN.   Chalets on clifftop.

BEVIN.   I'm hopin'.

OLD BEVIN.   Be shot of the cows.

BEVIN.   Bugger the cows.

OLD BEVIN.   Bugger Sir Dennis.

BEVIN.   Aye, bugger 'un.

They return to their flask. A CHAUFFEUR *appears, followed at a distance by an old lady. The labourers do not react.*

CHAUFFEUR.   Wotcha, mates. *(He stands uncomfortably, flexing and unflexing a gloved fist.)* All right, leaving the motor out there? *(They take no notice.)* No tractors or nothin'? No combine harvesters doing the ton? Don't fancy no local colour on me coachwork. No dents in me wax, right? *(Pause.)* Chicken feathers round the wipers? *(Pause.)* Etcetera. *(The old lady stops beside him.)*

MRS BRAYBON.   Ask them how much they are paid.

CHAUFFEUR.   Sorry?

MRS BRAYBON.   Their earnings. What are they?

CHAUFFEUR.   Right. *(He flexes uncomfortably.)*

MRS BRAYBON *(to herself, as she looks round).*   In here, did it happen? His first sin? On some mossy tomb, his fingers stealing across the holiday-tanned flesh? The khaki shorts gaping, all invitation? The vile country, thick with scent and powdery pollen, rotting like urine and dung . . .

CHAUFFEUR *(to the labourers).*   Not what you'd call a hefty whack, is it? Not a Bacardi drinker's vision of paradise, I suspect? What is it? Five fivers? Not pryin' or nothin'. Watcha make, lads, may I ask?

MRS BRAYBON *(still to herself).*   Holding this place in his heart, licking his memory for some soppy sentiment. Tears in his eyes for a murmur of England. HP sauce got him weeping. I heard.

CHAUFFEUR *(to her).*   No luck.

MRS BRAYBON.   I will have to talk to them.

CHAUFFEUR.   Yup.

MRS BRAYBON.   Have to bargain with them.

CHAUFFEUR.   Sorry.

He shrugs. She goes to the labourers, who do not look up.

MRS BRAYBON.   Do you know what is in this bag?

OLD BEVIN.   Sh'ud need x-ray eyes to tell 'ee, sh'udn't I?

BEVIN.   Us ain't Batman, is us, pop?

MRS BRAYBON.   A heart. My son's heart. *(Pause.)*

OLD BEVIN.   Is that so?

MRS BRAYBON.   It has travelled nearly three thousand miles. In a box. He wanted it buried here.

OLD BEVIN.   Peculiar.

BEVIN.   Most folks is fallin' arse over tit to get shot of 'ere.

MRS BRAYBON.   I wouldn't blame them. But my son wasn't normal. He was an intellectual and thought that excused him everything. He was wrong. He was quite simply bad-mannered, badly-dressed and unpatriotic. Will you dig a hole for it? *(The labourers look at one another.)* I ask because it isn't possible to go through the formalities. The printed matter. Vicar. Christ and so on. Neither possible nor relevant. I will pay you double your week's wages. *(They cogitate.)*

OLD BEVIN.   How deep a hole?

MRS BRAYBON.   You advise me.

BEVIN.   Keep out foxes. . . .

OLD BEVIN.   Damned difficult. Flints an' that.

BEVIN.   Deep 'ole.

OLD BEVIN.   'Ave to be.

BEVIN.   Damned deep 'ole, I reckon . . .

CHAUFFEUR *(sarcastically).*   Yeah, well try not to damage Australia.

OLD BEVIN.   Hundred pound.

CHAUFFEUR.   One hundred!

MRS BRAYBON *(opening her bag).*   At night. And in silence. No one to know. *(She counts out ten new notes, gives them to* OLD BEVIN, *then she removes a simple casket and hands it to him. He pops it in his lunch bag.)*

MRS BRAYBON *(to herself.)*   I think I should kiss it. Not for sentiment. But to impress them. So when my back is turned, they don't just feed it to some pigs. *(She looks at them.)* Would you mind giving it back a moment? Please? *(*OLD BEVIN *rummages it out, hands it to her. She kisses it, closing her eyes, then gives it back and walks away.)*

CHAUFFEUR.   Not a bad ol' life, eh? Birds singin' an' a straw in yer gob. *(They ignore him.)* Ta ta. *(He goes out. They begin eating sandwiches. Pause.)*

BEVIN.   Diggin' no bloody 'ole, is thee? *(Pause.)* Gi' it sow for 'a breakfast *(Pause.)*

OLD BEVIN.   Her boy, ain't it?

BEVIN.   Aye so.

OLD BEVIN.   Well . . . *(Pause.)*

BEVIN.   Diggin' nothin'. *(Pause.)*

OLD BEVIN.   Fond of 'un. 'As kissed it.

BEVIN.   Saw 'a. *(Pause.)*

OLD BEVIN.   Must bury it.

BEVIN.   Soft, 'ee are.

OLD BEVIN.   Mebbe. But us got ta bury it. *(Pause. With a shrug,* BEVIN *switches on a transistor radio.)*

Scene Two

A plain room in H.M.Prison. A desk with a chair at either end, on which is placed a milk bottle containing dead flowers. The door opens, a man wearing a striped suit and a bow tie comes in. The door closes. The man replaces the dead flowers with a bunch of his own, tosses the dead ones into the bin. He sits, hands folded in his lap. After a while, the door opens, a youth appears, dressed in prison blue. The door closes. The youth sits in the empty chair staring at the floor.

DIVER.   You're my criminal.

STOAT.   MP aren't cha, sir?

DIVER.   Yes.

STOAT.   Flattered, sir.

DIVER.   You may look at me. If you wish.

STOAT.   Can't sir.

DIVER.   Call me Tom.

STOAT.   Tom.

DIVER.   What are you here for?

STOAT.   Killed a queer. Tom.

DIVER.   Do you like my flowers?

STOAT.   Delphiniums.

DIVER.   Spot on.

STOAT.   The scent.

DIVER.   I do wish you'd look at me.

STOAT.   Yeah.

DIVER.   Something wrong with my face?

STOAT.   Don't know. Can't see it.

DIVER.   Well, you only have to —

STOAT.   No offence. Just don't. Never have done.

DIVER.   Extraordinary.

STOAT.   Dad's the same. An' mum. Funny house.

DIVER.   The floor's so ugly.

STOAT.   Must be why I like mosaics.

DIVER.   Very good . . .

STOAT.   Should 'ave lived in Pompeii.

DIVER.   Yes . . . very funny . . . very good . . .

STOAT.   I have me moments.

DIVER.   Read much?

STOAT.   Botany.

DIVER.   Botany?

STOAT.   On me papers, ain't it?

DIVER.   I never read them. Prefer to chat. I have an inbuilt resistance to officialdom. Reports, enquiries, white papers and what not, are no substitute for conversation. I speak as a journalist, of course. I thrive on gossip. Do you collect specimens?

STOAT.   Pressing, you mean?

DIVER.   Have a book, do you? A flower book?

STOAT.   Murder, ain't it?

DIVER.   Of a sort.

STOAT.   Pressing to death. Medieval torture, wasn't it? Flowers have got feelings.

DIVER.   Now that is interesting —

STOAT.   I killed a queer. *(Pause.)* I mean, you knew that, did you? Tom?

DIVER.   Yes. You don't have to go on about it. Not to me.

STOAT.   Boring you, am I?

DIVER.   That subject.

STOAT.   I am boring.

DIVER.   I don't agree.

STOAT.   I am. To you. If you were honest. I don't see why you come here. Why do you people visit? When you have witty friends and that. Why bore yerself?

DIVER.   You are witty. And a friend, I hope. In the making.

STOAT.   Got to be honest, Tom. Flattery's dead boring. *(Pause.)*

DIVER.   Sorry. Yes. *(Pause.)* I come because I believe society is a community and involvement is the essence of community. That is why I am a socialist. *(Pause.)* I also visit old ladies. I am painting an eighty year old's flat in Hammersmith. It is not even my constituency. She is crippled by arthritis.

STOAT.   What colour?

DIVER.   Magnolia.

STOAT.   Hate cultivated flowers. Vulgarity. God made plenty of flowers. Didn't need to interfere with 'em.

DIVER.   Interesting point.

STOAT.   Like Rolls Royces. Vulgar. Like them lapdogs. Can't hardly breathe or walk. Get heart attack if they raise a leg. Makes pissing a gamble when there're so highly bred. I'd drown 'em. I'd drown all artificial things. Simpleness is everything.

DIVER.   There is a danger of generalizing though, isn't there? I mean, I would agree that Rolls Royces are an obscenity, whilst bearing in mind their export potential, which in turn can earn us money for socially beneficial things, but to take an orchid — it can overwhelm you, can't it? *(Pause.)* I think. Can move you. Profoundly move you. *(Pause.)* I am a bit of a sensualist. . . . *(Pause.)* Perhaps more than a bit. . . .

STOAT.   Posh for a socialist. Snobby for a socialist.

DIVER.   Wilde was a socialist.

STOAT.   Who?

DIVER.   Oscar.

STOAT.   Funny. Bent toffs being socialists. In their big houses, sniffing one another's frilly cuffs an' that.

DIVER.   There are two paths to socialism. Indignation and sensibility. Both legitimate. There is even a third, which is logic. But I don't care for that.

Pause. He looks at STOAT *for a while.* STOAT *suddenly gets up.*

STOAT.   See you again, shall I?

DIVER.   Yes.

STOAT.   I don't bore yer?

DIVER.   No. I hope I don't bore you.

STOAT.   Not much.

He goes and knocks on the door. It opens, and he goes out. DIVER *takes out a cigarette and lights it.*

DIVER *(to himself.)* Oh, dear . . . *(Pause. He smiles.)* Sometimes I have to admit the very slightest sense of shame. Even now. When shame is almost redundant. When you are sixty-four and shame is like pyjamas, neatly-folded, in a drawer with mothballs, put away. There in case you go to hospital, but worn — never! And to admit you feel it is to admit you have never escaped, and never really want to, but that it clings there in some deep pore like sweat, like socialism, prickling the follicles when you're hot, rising in the midst of cocktails, unexpectedly, making you suddenly want to smash a glass. Childish, but impossible to eradicate. . . . *(Pause.)* Botany. Must brush up on botany. *(He gets up. A warder comes in.)*

WARDER.   Oh, I'm sorry, Tom.

DIVER.   Sorry? Why? He was charming in his way.

WARDER.   The arm band. Didn't notice it when you came in. *(He indicates the black arm band.)*

DIVER.   Oh, yes. An old friend of mine. He died in Russia.

WARDER.   Long way from home.

DIVER.   No. It was his home. He liked it.

WARDER.   Well, every man to his own.

DIVER.   Exactly. *(He starts to go out.)*

WARDER.   See you next week, then?

DIVER.   Oh yes, I think so. *(Pause.)* Yes.

WARDER *(holding the door for him).*   Take it easy. All that voting in the lobbies. Up and down the carpets. Ayes and Noes.

DIVER.   It's **too** fatiguing, love . . . *(They both laugh. DIVER goes out.)*

Scene Three

The churchyard gates. The CHAUFFEUR is helping MRS BRAYBON into a car. A VICAR appears.

MOSCROP.   And what did you make of the tympanum?

CHAUFFEUR.   Wha'?

MOSCROP.   The tympanum. Christ appearing to Saint Sebastian.

CHAUFFEUR.   Sorry. Wha'?

MOSCROP.   What they all flock here for. What the vultures gather for.

CHAUFFEUR.   No fanks. *(He starts to move again.)*

MOSCROP.   Someone tried to urinate on it. From the horizontal. Not possible of course, unless in possession of an outrageous bladder. It wasn't why we put the canvas over it. That was the ultra-violet. It was fading. After four-hundred years and the fixed stares of globe-trotting Japanese.

CHAUFFEUR *(pausing).*   Yeah. *(He bends to MRS BRAYBON'S feet.)*

MOSCROP.   Saint Sebastian is the treasure.

MRS BRAYBON.   Well, go and guard it. *(To CHAUFFEUR)* No, lift my feet. **Lift** them.

MOSCROP.   Coach loads from Düsseldorf to see him.

MRS BRAYBON.   My ankles are not flexible. That is the entire problem. Were they flexible, I should not need your help, should I?

CHAUFFEUR.   No.

MOSCROP.   Ex-Nazis. SS Generals with a partiality for art. Having blown down half of Europe, they understandably adore the peaceful atmosphere.

CHAUFFEUR.   Sorry . . .

MOSCROP.   Not that their appetite for looting has abated one tiny bit. Only now they offer Deutschmarks. Who needs a Flammenwerfer when you have a cheque book?

CHAUFFEUR *(having secured* MRS BRAYBON'S *feet).*   All aboard.

MOSCROP.   We have our Nazis here, of course. **One died this week.**

MRS BRAYBON.   What is the matter with this man?

CHAUFFEUR.   Search me.

MOSCROP.   Talk to me. There is no one to talk to here!

MRS BRAYBON.   That's the penalty of living in the country.

MOSCROP.   I didn't want to. It was for my nerves.

MRS BRAYBON.   I don't think it's worked.

MOSCROP.   Sir Dennis was a **Nazi.** Shhh! *(He grins weakly.)* The tower is two hundred and eighteen feet high, of shingled stone, the finials restored by a Mr Barry, rather poorly, in 1889. **Do you want to know about it.** Shhh.

MRS BRAYBON.   No. We are driving to Surrey.

MOSCROP.   Don't.

MRS BRAYBON.   You aren't well.

MOSCROP.   That's right.

MRS BRAYBON.   You are delirious.

MOSCROP.   Drowned in his own pond. The day before yesterday. Won a VC in the war. At Anzio. They're making the memorial at this minute but does it say — the nave is one hundred and forty-seven feet in length — he used his estate for **blackshirt training** — Shh! *(He looks at her. Pause.)*

CHAUFFEUR *(at the wheel).*   Shall we scoot, then?

MRS BRAYBON.   People were funny between the wars . . .

MOSCROP.   **Does it say?**

MRS BRAYBON.   You're supposed to be a priest, aren't you? You know about shame. Do we have to uncover every blemish? The grave is a fit place for flattery. Never mind the rest. *(The* CHAUFFEUR *starts the car.)*

MOSCROP.   I no longer believe in God.

MRS BRAYBON.   Me neither.

MOSCROP.   I cannot find it in me to forgive.

MRS BRAYBON.   Everything. I forgive everything but disloyalty. To be a blackshirt is an aberration, to be a communist is disloyalty. To your people, to the womb. I forgive everything but that.

MOSCROP.   That isn't really fair, is it?

CHAUFFEUR.   Okay?

MOSCROP.   I have to disagree with you.

MRS BRAYBON.   Drive off.

MOSCROP.   Patriotism is not the property of the —

The CHAUFFEUR *gives two quick blasts of the horn.* MOSCROP *steps back, and the car pulls away. He looks after it a moment. The* BEVINS *walk slowly past, the transistor radio hanging from* BEVIN's *scythe.*

OLD BEVIN.   Day t'yer.

MOSCROP.   You know — *(OLD BEVIN stops. BEVIN plods on.)* You know, what I have to appreciate in Christ appearing to Saint Sebastian is that the men who painted it were — labourers. *(OLD BEVIN looks at him.)* The cancer of specialisation had not been forced on the community by capital. *(pause.)*

OLD BEVIN.   Ar . . .

MOSCROP.   The division of labour, you see. On the one hand artists, on the other, clods.

OLD BEVIN.   Ar . . .

MOSCROP.   Get you a ladder, shall I? Go up with a pot of Dulux. Paint England as you see it. Fancy it?

OLD BEVIN.   No, zur.

MOSCROP.   Clod Art.

OLD BEVIN.   Zur?

MOSCROP.   Would the Audis and the Opels cruise our lanes for that? Wedge their Mercedes in the lych-gate for a glimpse of that?

OLD BEVIN.   No, zur.

MOSCROP.   They would not. They certainly would not.

OLD BEVIN.   Foreigners is all right, zur. Pays their way, don't 'em? An' more on top. 'Em don't know a pound from a shillin', does they, zur?

MOSCROP.   I see you're no petty-minded xenophobe, Bevin.

OLD BEVIN.   Zur?

MOSCROP.   The Common Market spirit's **got to you.** *(OLD BEVIN* *shrugs, ambles away.)* Oh, this mean, degraded place, this semi-feudal shit-heap, crawling with cretins and speculating squires . . .

KAREN.   Psst! *(He looks round, sees nothing.)* Psst! *(A skinny girl of about 15 appears, wearing a faded mini-skirt.)* 'As 'a gone? My 'usband an' the ol' man? Gone 'as 'a?

MOSCROP.   Yes.

KAREN.   Mister Moscrop, you 'ave gotta 'elp me.

MOSCROP.   Have I?

KAREN.   Oh, yes, you 'ave.

MOSCROP.   Why?

KAREN.   'nother baby. *(Pause.)*

MOSCROP.   Ah.

KAREN.   'll kill me. My 'usband'll kill me.

MOSCROP.   Oh, I think that's taking rather a dim view of —

KAREN.   You did Mrs Guntrip. *(Pause. He stares at her.)* You did.

MOSCROP.   If you do not want the baby, you must see the doctor.

KAREN.   Seen 'um. Says I got no grounds.

MOSCROP.   Then I don't see how I can —

KAREN.   You did Mrs Guntrip. She 'ad no grounds.

MOSCROP.   Please. Shh.

KAREN.   Got to do me, thun.

MOSCROP.   Haven't **got** to do anything.

KAREN.   Not movin' till you promise. *(Pause.)*

MOSCROP.   I was going to suggest — I had a word with Mr Bevin — but perhaps —

KAREN.   No. Only likes pop music. *(Pause.)*

MOSCROP.   All right.

KAREN.   Y'are a good vicar, y'are. Believe in Gard, I do.

MOSCROP.   No need for that.

KAREN.   I do, honest I do.

MOSCROP.   All right. Shove off! *(He turns away from her.)*

KAREN.   Be round on Tuesday. Come ta vicarage . . . *(She hesitates, goes out.)*

MOSCROP.   John Constable was a liar. He did not paint rick-burning and the hanging of rebels. Man-traps or cholera in brown water. He would not show that ignorant stillness can rise up, and for one brief moment in the flame-light the ugly become beautiful!

Scene Four

A table in the Cafe Royal. DIVER *sits with* SLAUGHTERFORD, *a Fleet Street crony, and* SLESS, *an Irish surgeon. All three wear black armbands.*

SLESS.   I circumcised him. He was thirty-three. I said this is an operation, which if you want it, you should have at three months. He said, at three months I was not consulted, and if I had have been, I should have had to say, the appearance of this organ is of supreme indifference to me, not entirely grasping the scope of its functions at the time, and the aesthetic prejudices with which the poor thing was likely to come into conflict. After that, I did his tonsils, because his breath smelled. And he was booked in for a colotomic survey when he did the bunk. The first indication of his whereabouts, you may remember, was the telegram from Moscow which said thank you, he did no longer need the bed. *(He bursts out laughing.)*

SLAUGHTERFORD.   I interviewed his mother, the day the story broke. She had hung a Union Jack above the porch and the National Anthem was playing on a gramophone. She had got a servant to stand there and replace the needle when it ended. We were crowded in the hallway. Tom was there, for the Observer. And she came out in a white dress, much too young for her, and said I have a statement for the press. God save the Queen. Long live the Empire. Perish all traitors. There was a bit of shifting feet. I was the first to ask a question, having been a friend of George. I said, deliberately naive this, did it come as a surprise to you to find your son had been for twenty years a communist? She said, she was an actress — a tenth-rate film actress — given his parents it would have been positively indecent had the art of dissimulation not come naturally. His father was a city swindler, you see. *(They all burst out laughing.)*

DIVER.   I took him to a football match. He had never seen one, though they had made him play rugby at school. He arrived wearing a supporters' scarf and bobble cap, though not associated with either of the clubs we were watching. Brand new, these were, and a spotless rattle. People did use rattles then. Even Harrods stocked them. We stood far down the terrace in the thick of the abuse and unsolicited fair comment. The supporter standing next to him was particularly vehement in urging a certain player to 'kick the bastards in the crutch.' After this one remark had been yelled right through into injury time and the final whistle had been blown, George turned to him and said, 'There comes a time when too great an attachment to a single idea renders one intensely bloody boring.' And the man just looked at him, blinking slowly. When we got outside, George said he fully expected the man to hit him, and was rather disappointed to find yet further evidence of the ingrained habit of deference in the working man, which had made the fellow silent in the face of George's accent. *(They all laugh.)*

Scene Five

The churchyard at night. BEVIN *and* OLD BEVIN *appear pressed close to the wall.* OLD BEVIN *has a spade.*

BEVIN.   A don't like it, pop . . .

OLD BEVIN.   Wha'?

BEVIN.   Ain't never cum 'ere after dark.

OLD BEVIN.   Soft git.

BEVIN.   Down 'ere, wha's wrong with 'ere?

OLD BEVIN.   Anywhere'll do, A s'pose. . . .

BEVIN.   T'is ground, t'is sacred, aren't it?

OLD BEVIN.   Well stand away from soddin' spade —

BEVIN.   Wha's tha'!

OLD BEVIN.   Christ Almightly, thou art a ninny! Put down the casket, put yer earplug in an' listen to yar soddin' music! All this jumpin' like a —

BEVIN.   Cum on, dig it an' less get 'ome!

OLD BEVIN *(sinking the spade).*   Coupla feet'll do a, she won't know different, will sha'?

Scene Six

Inside the church. MOSCROP, *in an overall, is placing a long ladder against the spandrel of an arch in the nave. In the light of a powerful torch the centuries old lines of a painting appear, vague and worn.* MOSCROP *kneels and opens a can of household paint. Then he climbs the ladder with it, and at the top, dips in a brush and with a gesture of conviction, makes the first bold stroke across the tympanum.*

Scene Seven

The churchyard. OLD BEVIN *is digging.* BEVIN, *holding the casket in one hand, is twirling the dials of his transistor with the other, a strange expression on his face.*

BEVIN.   Whassa . . . allo . . . allo . . . s'na Junny Cash, s'na . . . wha' . . .

He looks to see that OLD BEVIN *has stopped digging and his face too is taut with listening. The sound of 'Libera Me' chorus of Britten's 'War Requiem' rises slowly to its crescendo, and as it does so the* BEVINS *stare with horror into the tombstones, which are tinted with a peculiar light. Coming towards them from the war memorial, moving with slow steps, are the ghosts of the village war dead, led by* LT.COL.ST.LEGER, VC, *holding his sword in front of him. Behind him, chiefly of the First World War, come infantrymen in mud-encrusted uniform, and one in desert kit. Their unearthly gait brings them to where the* BEVINS *crouch in terror.*

BEVIN.   Can't move, pop . . . can't move. . . !

Mouthing silently, the ghosts crowd round them as the quieter movement of the music begins. Their mouths work in their struggle to speak.

ST LEGER.   My village. . . . My village. . . . My village. . . .

SMITH *(staring at* OLD BEVIN*).*   Jack . . . Jack . . . tha raises us from our sleep, tha ol' bastard thee. . . .

ST LEGER.   My village. . . . My village. . . .

JONES.   Jack, tha never cum with us, dids't tha? Tha sneaks't tha way into Reserved Occupation, didn't thee?

ST LEGER.   My village. . . . My village. . . .

SMITH.   Dids' na die with us, dids't tha? On soddin' beach at Anzio?

OLD BEVIN.   Someone 'ad ta keep farms goin', didn't tha?

JONES.   We forgive 'ee, Jack, on that score. Don't fret, lad . . .

ST LEGER.   Village. . . . Village. . . .

BROWN *(indicating* ST LEGER*).*   Squire's father, as fell at Loos, says boys t'is Bevin as is buryin' a traitor in our midst, as layin' an enemy of the queen in the churchyard none of us cud lie in.

ST LEGER.   My village. . . . My village. . . .

SMITH.   Shame on 'ee, Jack, for us who got done for our country!

OLD BEVIN.   A didn't know — did A. We didn't know —

DEAD BEVIN.   Lad, A last saw thee as a baby —

OLD BEVIN *(as the soldier in desert uniform moves forward).*   Dad! Who fell in Palestine!

DEAD BEVIN.   Aye, died at th' hand of the terrible Turk, for freein' Holy Places —

OLD BEVIN.   M'old Dad. M'ol' Dad!

DEAD BEVIN.   Defile ma memory with th' 'eart, mouldy old 'eart in casket, an' ma gran'son 'elpin' thee, oh, Jack!

ST LEGER.   Shame on vile traitors in our midst! Look to thyself, England! St Leger and England, ho!

SMITH/BROWN/JONES.   **St Leger an' England, ho!**

OLD BEVIN.   We did na know son, did we? Did we know? *(*BEVIN *shakes his head in terror.)*

SMITH.   Jack, when we look at thee, we see that wars took best, an' left ol' rubbish, didn't 'em?

ST LEGER.   **St Leger and England, ho!**

EDWARDS.   Broke our sleep, ol' bugger, for 'undred quid!

ST LEGER *(pointing his sword).*   **Kill! Kill! There is the enemy! Kill!**

JONES.   Piss on Bevins.

SMITH.   Hang thyself!

DEAD BEVIN.   In barn, do thyself an injury!

OLD BEVIN.   Dad, yer can't mean as A sh'ud — *(They groan in chorus, drowning him.)*

BEVIN.   Fock th' heart!

He kicks the casket violently. Suddenly the dead are silent, still. A figure dressed in a shabby Russian fur hat and coat appears. He walks slouchingly towards them, stops. A pause.

BRAYBON.   George Braybon. *(Pause.)* I — *(Pause.)* Not the most persuasive speaker in the world. What with stutter. *(Pause.)* Nor is it easy, off the cuff, to give curriculum vitae of one's political ideology. *(Pause.)* So briefly. Point I want to make is, that this place is Heaven to me. *(Pause.)* No. Not being honest. Sorry. Don't mean England's Heaven, I mean this spot, this corner, for reasons much too personal to enter into now —

ST LEGER.   **St Leger and England, ho!**

BRAYBON.   My d-d-d-defection, my celebrated d-d-d-defection, was not treason to the place, but to its governors —

ST LEGER *(pointing his sword).*   **There is the enemy!**

BRAYBON.   Shut up, will you? I am trying to speak. *(There is a low, continuous groan from the dead.)* I am trying to d-d-d-differentiate between partriotism in its perverted form and love of country, because — *(The groan gets louder.)* whether you believe me or not, I don't care how you bleat, there is a loyalty higher than loyalty to your bloody governors — I know that must be d-d-d-damned difficult to grasp — a loyalty, if you will listen — to yourselves — a loyalty which d-d-d-demands a minimum of wit and even — *(The groaning is deafening, BRAYBON shrugs his shoulders.)* Oh God, the bloody English yob. The bloody world-historical English yob. . . . *(Seeing their opportunity, the BEVINS grab up the shovel and dash out of the churchyard, leaving the racket behind.)*

Scene Eight

The Cafe Royal.

SLAUGHTERFORD.   He was certain they were onto him. In the middle fifties, after Suez.. Something got leaked through an embassy. Or something. They had him up at Whitehall for a grilling. He went up to the office and the investigator or whatever — did he ever tell you this — was a woman. And he said he felt affronted. That they hadn't sent him to a man. Whilst accepting, as a communist, the equality of women, he felt affronted. Because in England, of course, not being a free society, and women, not being, so to speak, fully utilized, it was technically to undervalue him. He argued, anyway. But having got him there, she gave him hell you see. Skinned him. All but cracked him. And he said — he must have told you this — at the end of it, he proposed to her. *(They burst out laughing.)* No, listen, listen. Because, he said, although I am not partial to women, and have not properly consummated the notorious and grossly overestimated act, I never felt the desire to cohabit till now. Such was his repsect for her, his predilections were scattered to the winds. To which she replied, how it was typical of men, that the only thing they could think of doing to a woman who outwitted them was marry and put them on the mantelpiece.

SLESS.   He had no faith in Russian hospitals. He dreaded illness over there. He told me he kept a capsule underneath his pillow, so if he woke up with something serious, he would be spared the attentions of their doctors. But the problem was that every time he woke up, he felt rotten. It was habitual with him. So he was forever handling the capsule, but never swallowed it. How do you know when you're dying, he asked me, you have no information to go on. It isn't like Chablis, that you know at the first sip if the bottle is off. *(Pause.)* He begged me never to let on what he thought of their hospitals. He did not want his squeamishness used by their enemies.

DIVER.   Chablis was not his favourite wine. Talking of Chablis. He reckoned he had tasted only one decent bottle — *(Suddenly he is aware of the figure of* BRAYBON, *in the same fur coat and hat, trying to attract his attention.* DIVER *stares, but carries on speaking.)* In a supermarket in Kursk. I don't know what he was doing in Kursk. Not looking for Chablis. He had a case of Château Mouton —

BRAYBON.   **Tom! Tom!**

DIVER.   Monthly order from Harrods . . . the Special Branch wanted to poison it . . . but the Minister overruled . . .

BRAYBON.   **They won't let me lie there, d-d-d-**

DIVER.   On the grounds that no bottle of vino could thereafter be trusted . . . the KGB would retaliate . . . would kill the wine trade dead . . .

BRAYBON.   **Damned peasants!**

SLESS *and* SLAUGHTERFORD *laugh at* DIVER's *story; one of them tells another anecdote.*

DIVER *(to* BRAYBON*)*   Where — I —

BRAYBON.   **Our church, Tom!**

DIVER.   Where was — I —

BRAYBON.   **Our church, bloody hell!**

DIVER.   Fuddled, you see, this drinking — for you —

BRAYBON.   **St Enoch's!**

DIVER *(unconvincing)*.   God, yes.

BRAYBON.   **Nineteen – thirty – bloody – three.**

DIVER.   Was it?

BRAYBON.   Was it, he says. D-D-D-Dissembler!

DIVER.   They said you got bronchitis —

BRAYBON.   Got the heart to Mother. With directions. All right Moscow end. But she had to fluff it, silly bitch.

DIVER.   The **heart?** Your **heart?**

BRAYBON.   Kicked around the churchyard. My old ticker. Enlarged, with weak valve in left-ventricle. Dogsmeat rotten now, but my old ticker, which beat quicker in your company!

DIVER.   Tell me about Russia, George.

BRAYBON.   No.

DIVER.   Your flat. On the Nevsky Prospect, was it? No, that's Leningrad —

BRAYBON.   No.

DIVER.   I got the tie-pin. Thank you. Look, I'm wearing it. Corpus Christi rowing club.

BRAYBON.   May seem bloody d-d-d-daft to you, but I'm concerned about the **heart!**

DIVER.   I'm drunk.

BRAYBON.   I'm **dead!**

DIVER.   Yes. . . .

BRAYBON.   **Help me!**

DIVER *(trying to sit up straight)*.   Yes. I'm sorry. I'm sorry but I'm dribbling drunk.

BRAYBON.   Find it. Cherish it.

DIVER.   Got a Labour Party executive tomorrow and —

BRAYBON.   **Cherish it.**

DIVER.   Yes. *(Pause.)* Yes. George. *(*BRAYBON *goes.* DIVER *blinks into a form of normalcy.)*

SLESS.   He spent a day with Churchill. Did he tell you? After Munich. Churchill was laying bricks. Apparently he could not talk and lay a brick. So there were long silences. George said, during a silence, would Churchill mind if he had a go, and laid a brick. When the silence was over, Churchill said no. It was his damned wall and his damned bricks. So George said — this'll kill you — *(a burst of laughter.)*

Scene Nine

The churchyard. MOSCROP, *in his painting overall, is shining his torch around, having come out in response to the noise. The groaning fades.*

MOSCROP.   Who's there? Come on! Anyone? **Don't be silly!** *(He flashes the torch over the ground, picking out the casket. He turns it over with his foot, sees the contents. Instantly he switches off the torch.)* I'm armed! *(Pause.)* Been to the pictures? Seen The Exorcist have we? Gone to our silly little heads, has it? Because there is a God, there has to be a devil, does there? Because there is a devil, has to be a God? Oh, dear, oh, dear. **The squire was a Nazi!** Listening? If you want a devil. Haven't got that far to look . . . *(He switches on the torch again, picks up the casket, goes off.)*

Scene Ten

MRS BRAYBON'S *house. Sitting at a table*, MRS BRAYBON, *the* CHAUFFEUR, DIVER, *playing snap.*

MRS BRAYBON.   The mothers of the other traitors coddled them. Shut their doors and drew the curtains. They had no sap. I called the press here. I said George is a traitor to his nation, to his class, and to his school. Not that he liked his school, but he liked his class, for all his communism.

CHAUFFEUR.   Snap!

MRS BRAYBON.   They scuttled to the East for secret holidays. The mothers of the others. On the Black Sea, is it? Or met their sons in Swiss hotels. I did not see George. Or send him hampers. I did not stroke him. He always knew exactly where he stood with me. To me he died. He might have been missing in some air-raid over Germany.

CHAUFFEUR.   Snap!

MRS BRAYBON.   Except he was not a pilot.

CHAUFFEUR.   Snap!

MRS BRAYBON.   No. That is the four of hearts.

CHAUFFEUR.   Oh, yeah.

MRS BRAYBON.   George was too clever for his own good. I don't know where he got his brains from. Not from me. I would not have wished him brains. He would have done better dying over Germany.

DIVER.   He did valuable work in the war. For MI5.

MRS BRAYBON.   Yes. Drinking himself silly in the country.

DIVER.   Yes. They had some good times.

MRS BRAYBON.   When your country is at war, the decent men are in uniform.

DIVER.   He had a uniform. He just never wore it.

MRS BRAYBON.   Exactly.

CHAUFFEUR.   Snap!

MRS BRAYBON.   You were in uniform, weren't you?

DIVER.   I was at the Ministry of Information.

MRS BRAYBON.   **I am not a crank. And I loved him. They accused me of not loving him. But love gives way. It is not the sole virtue.**

DIVER.   He's dead now. Poor George.

MRS BRAYBON.   His lungs.

DIVER.   It was that, was —

MRS BRAYBON/CHAUFFEUR.   Snap!

CHAUFFEUR.   After you.

MRS BRAYBON.   His lungs.

DIVER.   Went, did they?

MRS BRAYBON.   According to them. I expect they poisoned him.

DIVER.   And why should they do that? I wonder?

MRS BRAYBON.   He was coming back. *(Pause. DIVER is puzzled, cautious.)*

DIVER.   Oh?

MRS BRAYBON.   Oh, yes.

DIVER.   Go on.

MRS BRAYBON.   No one leaves this country without wanting to come back. Not like Jamaica or Pakistan. They don't want to go back. But an Englishman, wherever he is, there is an aching to come back.

DIVER.   He liked the countryside. Water colours.

MRS BRAYBON. More than that.

DIVER. Oh?

MRS BRAYBON. Like some criminal skulking in South America, rabid for a bit of English company. Even to go to gaol, they come back. Because prison in England is preferable to freedom in exile. George would have enjoyed an English gaol. With his habits. Would have been drinking with the governor.

DIVER. I wonder how you can be so certain when you weren't — *(His cards have gone.)* I seem to be out. *(He lifts his hands.)* When you weren't in contact with him?

CHAUFFEUR. Lend yer some.

DIVER. It's all right.

CHAUFFEUR *(Bisecting his pack).* Here y'are.

DIVER. No, really, it's all right — *(The cards are put down before him. He takes them up.)*

MRS BRAYBON. George believed — snap! *(She collects a few.)* They'd let him back. Whenever he felt like it. Because they were his friends, you see. He was under the impression that Eton and Cambridge mattered more than treason. He was a very snobbish kind of red. The only place he liked the workers was in bed.

CHAUFFEUR. Snap! *(He looks at* DIVER *as he picks the cards up.)* You're not lookin'.

MRS BRAYBON. He had a longing to be a national hero. That is why he sent his heart back. When all the world is communist, he supposed the public would want to pay respect. Name pubs after him. For all his Moscow posturing, he liked the patriotic sod . . . *(She stops playing, looks at him.)* Do you know St Enoch's? *(Pause.)* I mean was it you, don't I?

CHAUFFEUR. Play.

MRS BRAYBON. Brown legs on the tombstone. Were yours.

CHAUFFEUR. Anyone? *(Pause.)*

DIVER. You see . . . I've actually forgotten . . . where St Enoch's is . . .

MRS BRAYBON. He hadn't.

DIVER. No. *(Pause.)*

CHAUFFEUR. Look, am I playin' on me tod?

Scene Eleven

Inside St. Enoch's. MOSCROP *is halfway through his modern primitive painting, 'The Clods Rise Up' which has a background of burning hayricks. St. Sebastian has virtually disappeared. Two tourists enter, peering around, whispering urgently.*

FIRST TOURIST.   Wo ist den grossische Oberfriegen?

SECOND TOURIST *(examining a guide).*   Er sagt, über die Slocht ist ein Tympanum . . .

FIRST TOURIST.   Ja . . .

SECOND TOURIST.   Warum ein primitif Sankte Sebastian, krank den aschen, versekt —

FIRST TOURIST.   Ein Tympanum . . . ein grosser Tympanum . . .

SECOND TOURIST *(moving up the aisle).*   Der Kristenfigur, beseekt von Lichtenfels und aber Hochenstrieff, ein Soldat liebt . . .

FIRST TOURIST *(calling to* MOSCROP, *on the ladder).*   Tympanum?

SECOND TOURIST.   Links, ein Fragenvater in rot und blau . . .

FIRST TOURIST.   Tympanum bitte?

MOSCROP.   The Clods Rise Up. *(He nods at his work.)*

FIRST TOURIST.   Bitte?

MOSCROP.   The Clods Rise Up. *(They stare up.)*

SECOND TOURIST.   Was ist das? *(*MOSCROP *paints on.)* Der Sankte Sebastian?

MOSCROP.   No.

SECOND TOURIST.   Nein?

MOSCROP.   Definitely nein. Saint Sebastian — kaput.

SECOND TOURIST *(to first).*   Er ist krank, nicht war?

MOSCROP *(pointing out his figures).*   The dumb speak. The illiterate are eloquent. The crude find grace.

FIRST TOURIST.   Bitte?

MOSCROP.   **Rebellion.** Constable would not paint it. So I have. *(They stare at him.)* **We are not quaint!**

Scene Twelve

The churchyard. STOAT *is examining a weed.* DIVER, *resting on a flat tombstone, is watching* STOAT.

DIVER. Good King Henry.... *(Pause.)* Chenopodium bonus-henricus . . .

STOAT. Nah . . .

DIVER. Surely.

STOAT. Never. S'Ol Geezer's Spit.

DIVER. What?

STOAT. S'what they call it.

DIVER. Ah.

STOAT. Or Piss Plant.

DIVER. Shall I look it up?

STOAT. Suit yerself. *(DIVER thumbs a pocket guide to English flora.)* Git a lot of it in graveyards.

DIVER. Piss or Spit?

STOAT *(looking up).* Wha'?

DIVER. Do I look it up under? *(Pause.)* You met my eyes.

STOAT *(going back to the weed).* Yeah. Well, accidents will happen. *(Pause.)*

DIVER. I had to work on this. This day out. They weren't keen.

STOAT. Gotta be rehabilitated, ain't I?

DIVER. Exactly what I told them. They could trust us.

STOAT. Yeah. Well, ta. *(Pause.)* I thought I had said ta. *(DIVER just watches him among the weeds.)*

DIVER. The sun on your hair . . .

STOAT. What about it?

BRAYBON. **Christ Almighty.** *(DIVER turns to see BRAYBON's ghost, still in the Russian furs, watching from a nearby grave.)* Cheap as ever. Read him a sonnet while you're at it.

DIVER. He's a botanist.

BRAYBON. Incorrigible Tom. Il Fellatio da Fleet Street.

DIVER. Graveyard. **Plenty of flowers. Though it might help him.** Rehabilitate. *(Pause.)* Though that's not all of it.

BRAYBON. Naturally not.

DIVER. Sorry, George.

BRAYBON. Get rid of him.

DIVER. I can't. Home Office standing orders. Got to be with him.

BRAYBON.   **Bloody hell!** *(Pause.* DIVER *turns to* STOAT*)*

DIVER.   Barry . . .

STOAT.   No.

DIVER.   No what?

STOAT.   Whatever you are askin'. *(Pause.)*

DIVER.   I would like some cigarettes.

STOAT.   Cigarettes?

DIVER.   Yes. Please. *(*STOAT *gets up, goes off. Pause.)*

BRAYBON.   Not sick for England, Tom. Propaganda. Saying I was sick for it.

DIVER.   Quite.

BRAYBON.   Not some engine-fitter in Australia saving for the boat home. Not some sentimental pom.

DIVER.   No, quite.

BRAYBON.   Put that about though, didn't they? George Braybon, lonely figure scuttling over Red Square for his Daily Telegraph.

DIVER.   Rather.

BRAYBON.   Weeping at bare mention of Oxford, Henley, Epsom, Cowes.

DIVER.   Yes.

BRAYBON.   England is not a list of place-names, Tom.

DIVER.   No.

BRAYBON.   Stuff Rupert Brooke.

DIVER.   Absolutely.

BRAYBON.   How could they do that to me?

DIVER.   You ask me!

BRAYBON.   **You did.**

DIVER.   Did I?

BRAYBON.   'In his spartan Moscow flat defector George Braybon reads *Little Dorrit* for the thirteenth time.' Express, 14th September, 1962.

DIVER.   You did read *Little Dorrit*.

BRAYBON.   Twenty times now.

DIVER.   There you are.

BRAYBON.   **What about my motives!**

DIVER. In reading Dickens?

BRAYBON. In **defecting.**

DIVER. Come on, George. No one would have published it. *(Pause.)* Got to live in the real world, George.

BRAYBON. This country isn't real.

DIVER. Maybe not. But there are still some damned good restaurants.

BRAYBON. Swallow your conscience with a d-d-d-decent Hock.

DIVER. Are you going to lecture me?

BRAYBON. When I left here I didn't give it ten more years. It was rancid. The sewers looked like choking on a century's accumulated rot. But ten years have brought nothing to relieve the jugged old bitch. The comic kingdom enters its lunatic phase. Yobs parading behind union jacks, proclaiming empires which would tickle the humour of a defenceless Kurd. Only now they wave the flag instead of wearing it on their backs or arses, like monkeys in some raucous independent state. Cant instead of Carnaby. History hasn't finished with the old bag yet, but wants to ridicule it before slitting its sagging throat. And that is your d-d-d-damned doing, d-d-d-dithering between the restaurant and party conference when you should have cleaned the body out before the rats got it. *(Pause.)* Poor old place. Obviously care for it, you see . . . Compromise and cynicism. Let the loonies in.

DIVER. I don't accept that as a fair description. Of my party. Just not revolutionary, that's all.

BRAYBON. D-D-D-Discover what is right. Then d-d-d-do it. *(Pause.)* Socrates.

DIVER. Well, I would go along with that. *(Pause.* BRAYBON *looks at him.)*

BRAYBON. **Have you found the bloody heart?**

DIVER. Ah —

BRAYBON. **Not looking!**

DIVER. We didn't actually have time to look —

BRAYBON. Got to be around here somewhere. **Got to be.**

DIVER *(stirring himself).* No one seems to cut the grass —

BRAYBON. Sent it to my mother, like an idiot. Try that way. Over there. (DIVER *moves methodically through the grass.)*

DIVER. What I was wondering . . . was why exactly . . . you should choose this spot . . . *(He stops.)* I mean . . . was it . . . *(Pause.)* Us? *(Pause.* BRAYBON *just looks at him.)* It was, was it? Ah . . .

BRAYBON *(Pointing to a flat gravestone).* On there.

DIVER.   I do remember.

BRAYBON.   **I do.**

DIVER.   19 — 19 —

BRAYBON.   36.

DIVER.   Yes. 36.

BRAYBON.   Put my hand out. Touched your leg.

DIVER.   That's right. *(Pause.)* Surprised me. *(Pause.)* Wasn't sure you ever would.

BRAYBON.   Me neither. But I had to. Terrible compulsion came along.

DIVER.   Naturally.

BRAYBON.   Not passion, though. I'm sorry. *(Pause.)* Bloody fascists at the gate. *(Pause.)*

DIVER.   What?

BRAYBON.   Blackshits. Marching past the bloody gate. Twirling some **humiliated jack.**

DIVER.   In **Devon?**

BRAYBON.   Half a dozen. Spotty clerks and butchers, glistening in the August sun.

DIVER.   In **Devon?**

BRAYBON.   I meant to tell you, afterwards. But afterwards, it seemed d-d-d-dishonest, out of keeping with the act, because I would not have done it had it not been for the blackshits. It was my first deliberate rebellion, Tom. And I liked it. And I've never stopped. *(Pause.)* Sorry. *(Pause.)* You're not hurt? *(Pause.)* I mean you didn't even recollect St Enoch's, did you? Don't pretend —

DIVER.   This would make a damned good story for a Sunday, George.

BRAYBON.   Botanist is coming back.

DIVER.   *Traitor's Tentative Treason.* Got to use those words. Newspaper jargon. No one attaches the slightest credibility to it. *Spy's Secret Sodomy.* Do you object?

BRAYBON.   Wholeheartedly.

DIVER.   But it would —

BRAYBON.   Missed my pun.

DIVER.   What?

BRAYBON.   Whole — **heart** — edly. Geddit?

DIVER.   Yes, very good, but —

BRAYBON. **Find it. Please.** *(He turns, starts to go.)*

DIVER. Look, George, what about this —

BRAYBON. **Find it, please!**

He disappears. STOAT *appears, with a packet of cigarettes.*

STOAT. Couldn't get no Turkish. Dunno what's happenin' to these corner stores.

DIVER. Thank you.

STOAT. **Shit!**

DIVER. What?

STOAT. Could've bunked off, couldn't I? Could 'ave been miles away by now.

DIVER. But you didn't.

STOAT. Must be round the twist, I reckon.

DIVER. Or was it something else? *(Pause.)* Barry? *(Pause.)* Were you perhaps, thinking of me? (STOAT *is looking uncomfortably at the ground.)* I shall always remember this afternoon. Always think of us together — *(He reaches out to touch* STOAT. *Suddenly there is a cry of panic.)*

FIRST TOURIST. Bitte! Bitte!

SECOND TOURIST. Entschuldigen sie! *(The* TOURISTS *are hurrying towards them, cameras flying.)*

FIRST TOURIST. Bitte! Bitte!

SECOND TOURIST *(gesticulating towards the church).* Der Pastor . . . er ist krank . . . sehr krank. . . !

DIVER *looks resigned,* STOAT *just stares at the ground.*

Scene Thirteen

Inside St Enoch's. MOSCROP *is up the ladder.* DIVER *enters, followed by the* TOURISTS *and* STOAT. *He walks up the aisle until he stands underneath the tympanum. Pause.*

DIVER. My German isn't what it used to be . . . *(Pause.)* They say you are defacing an historic monument . . . *(*MOSCROP *does not react. The* TOURISTS *rush up waving a guide book.)*

FIRST TOURIST. Das ist ein historische Piktur von dem Sankte Sebastian —

DIVER. Yes —

SECOND TOURIST.   Wir sind von Hamburg gekommen, den Sankte Sebastian zu sehen!

DIVER.   Yes.

STOAT *(gazing up at* MOSCROP's *effort).*   S'okay, ain't it — sort of — Day of Judgement punch-up — ain't it? Final Bundle, like . . .

DIVER *(to* MOSCROP).   I wonder if . . . has anybody handed in a heart?

FIRST TOURIST *(pulling* DIVER's *sleeve).*   Bitte . . . bitte . . . der Piktur . . .

STOAT *(rubbing his neck).*   Lookin' up there . . . strained me neck . . .

FIRST TOURIST.   Er ist ein Dummkopf, nicht war?

DIVER *(fending off).*   It is perfectly all right. I am on the Labour Party Executive. Leave everything to me. *(They look confused, take a final look at the tympanum, and shaking their heads, go out.)*

MOSCROP.   No more foreigners, feasting off the carcase, buying the people like black boys . . . *(Pause.)*

DIVER.   I was wondering, if anyone had handed in —

MOSCROP.   Yes. It's going off.

DIVER.   Off?

MOSCROP.   It smells.

DIVER.   I see . . . *(Pause.)* It belonged to a dear friend of mine. *(Pause.)* Who had a passion to be buried here. *(Pause.* MOSCROP *paints on.)*

MOSCROP.   An Englishman?

DIVER.   Yes.

MOSCROP.   We were flooded with offers from America a few years back. Vast endowments in exchange for picturesque graves under trees. Now it's Arabs, wanting damn great Muslim monuments. *(Pause.)* What happened to the rest of him?

DIVER.   He died in Moscow. *(Pause.)* He was George Braybon.

MOSCROP.   Ah.

DIVER. The traitor. *(Pause.)* So-called. *(Pause.)*

MOSCROP.   Wasn't he a traitor?

DIVER.   I suppose so, yes. *(Pause.* MOSCROP *is attentive to a stroke.)*

MOSCROP.   I cannot raise a stone to him. Much as I might like to.

DIVER.   No . . . *(Pause. He is puzzled but glad.)* I don't think he expected one.

MOSCROP.   I cannot because in a short time he will be a legend. There will be a tea-shop and a boutique full of souvenirs. Local people will be party to outrageous lies.

DIVER.   Quite.

MOSCROP.   And they rot so easily. *(He stops, wipes his hands, comes down the ladder a little way.)* People, I mean. With their feeble grasp on their integrity. *(DIVER nods as seriously as possible.)*

STOAT.   S'gone four.

MOSCROP.   It is a jungle here. It is not paradise.

STOAT.   Tom.

MOSCROP.   Braybon must have known it. The evil that comes swinging round a country lane. The peacock trained to cry Sieg Heil! *(He looks hard at DIVER.)*

STOAT.   Lose me soddin' remission if I'm late! *(DIVER is still staring at MOSCROP.)* Tom!

DIVER.   Yes . . . *(He smiles briefly.)* Got to go . . . *(He feels quickly for his wallet, takes out two notes.)* Will that cover the expenses? He only wants a little hole . . .

MOSCROP *takes the money.* DIVER *follows* STOAT *out.* MOSCROP, *wiping his hands, comes down the ladder, looks up at his work for a moment, then unties the cord which holds the canvas covering, letting it down over the tympanum. As he is walking out, a man comes in.*

ST LEGER.   I'm the new guvnor. *(He extends a hand.)* St Leger. How d'ya do? *(MOSCROP takes his hand.)* Guvnor's dead. Long live the guvnor. *(He grins.)* Not stopping. Just popped down for the funeral. Got a place in Albany. Won't see buggerall of me.

MOSCROP.   I should say I am sorry about Sir Dennis.

ST LEGER.   Old bat. Spare yerself th' hypocrisy.

MOSCROP.   But he was a blackshirt. *(Pause.)*

ST LEGER.   So he was. Like my uncle Donald. In fact I'm pretty well inclined that way myself.

MOSCROP.   Oh. Really.

ST LEGER.   Yup. *(Pause.)* Mind you, he chucked it up in '42.

MOSCROP.   The Blitz?

ST LEGER.   No. We had no London property. It was two Heinkels did it. Got lost on their way back from Swansea, blundered over the estate at tree-top level and ditched a load of phospherous bombs on his prize flock of Jacobs sheep. He joined the commandos next day. Got a VC down at Anzio.

MOSCROP.   So I believe.

ST LEGER.   Like me grandad.

MOSCROP.   All VCs.

ST LEGER.   S'right. Don't give 'em for rescuing merchant banks,
unfortunately. *(He grins.)* I'm off. Haven't set foot in here since I was
eleven. How's the treasure of the tympanum?

MOSCROP.   Much the same.

ST LEGER.   Mind if I take a look at it? *(MOSCROP shrugs. ST LEGER
walks up, unties the cord and pulls up the canvas cover. MOSCROP's
painting is revealed.)* You modern vicars . . . *(He grins, shakes his head,
lets the blind fall.)* See you in the morning. Cheers! *(He walks out.)*

Scene Fourteen

*A first class railway compartment. STOAT is sitting in one corner. DIVER,
behind a newspaper, lies along the length of the seat opposite. STOAT is lost
in thought for some time.*

STOAT.   Tom.

DIVER.   Yes?

STOAT.   Bin thinking. *(Pause. DIVER lowers the paper.)* Ain't coming
back to the Scrubs. *(DIVER lifts the paper again.)*

DIVER.   Silly.

STOAT.   Ain't.

DIVER.   Silly.

STOAT.   Don't keep saying that!

DIVER.   Unwise, then. When you're doing well. When I've put in so
much time for you. Ungrateful.

STOAT.   Plenty of ol' ladies left. Smelly lavs for you to paint.

DIVER.   Don't be cruel.

STOAT.   I'm abscondin'! *(Pause. DIVER folds the paper away.)*

DIVER.   I have taken an interest in you. I have cultivated your friendship.
And now you talk about betraying me. Very nice.

STOAT.   He did.

DIVER.   Who did?

STOAT.   Braybon or whatever his name was. The spy. Bunked off, didn't
he?

DIVER.   George was an idealist. He believed in something.

STOAT.   So do I.

DIVER.   What?

STOAT.   Freedom. *(Pause.)*

DIVER.   Yes. Well, you will get it. If you're patient.

STOAT.   **Gaol is 'orrible!**

DIVER.   Yes. Yes. But so is murder.

STOAT.   He took secrets to the Russians, didn't he? He was a criminal. He bunked off. But I don't 'ear you whine at him. He was an 'ero. Go about discussin' him. Like he was a proper character. I am a character. But I ain't from Eton, is that it? *(Pause.)*

DIVER.   You are very, very confused. Deeply, almost comically confused. But all the same I am delighted you can talk like this because it shows we're getting somewhere. There are billions of contradictions in what you're saying — the word freedom, for example, needs a bit of examining. But good, that you are talking like this, very good —

Suddenly STOAT *reaches up and pulls the communication cord. The brakes screech.*

STOAT.   Ta, ta, Tom.

DIVER *(rising to his feet).*   I will get into trouble for this!

STOAT*(opening the door).*   Risky business. Helping geezers in the nick. *(He jumps down onto the track.* DIVER *stands in the open door.)*

DIVER.   Hold it! Hold it! *(Pause. He stares after the running figure.)* Why don't we meet?

Scene Fifteen

The churchyard at St Enoch's. A funeral bell tolling. The BEVINS *stand some distance away, with shovels.* OLD BEVIN *jams on a hat.* ST LEGER *and a* WOMAN *stand by a grave.* MOSCROP *officiates.*

OLD BEVIN.   Sir Dennis be buried, thun.

BEVIN.   Aye.

OLD BEVIN.   New squire now, thun. What's cum up from London.

BEVIN.   'As fat arse on 'um.

OLD BEVIN.   Aye. All St Legers 'as fat arses.

BEVIN.   Cud bump against 'us missus.

OLD BEVIN.   Not 'us missus. 'As no missus.

BEVIN.   'Us tart, then. Cud steal 'er knickers.

OLD BEVIN.   Young bugger.

BEVIN.   Shall be orgies 'ere, now. Down at Manor.

OLD BEVIN.   Us won't be invited.

BEVIN.   Offic'ly.

OLD BEVIN.   Wha's tha' drivin' at?

BEVIN.   Can look through winders, can't us? Scramble up wisteria?

OLD BEVIN.   Better than Jack's film shows, tell 'ee.

BEVIN.   Cheaper, too . . .

ST LEGER *(picking up odd wreaths and reading the labels).*   Cheerio, Sir Dennis, Cocoa and two sugars, Lance-Corporal Dickie Wilson, formerly Batman, 1st Coy. Royal Marine Commandos, Salisbury, Rhodesia . . .

ZENA.   Ahhh . . . sweet . . .

ST LEGER *(picking up another).*   Dennis, you old fraud, it was **me** that was going to hold open the pearly gates for **you** . Aunt Jessica.

ZENA.   Oh, that's lovely! That's so sweet!

They move further from the grave as they pick up wreaths. MOSCROP, *still at the edge of the grave, slips his hand beneath his cassock and takes out the casket containing* BRAYBON's *heart. Surreptitiously, he drops it in the hole.*

ST LEGER *(reading still).*   Have a double waiting for us, Dennis. Sorely missed. New Zealand St Legers.

ZENA.   Get around, don't they?

ST LEGER.   To a Proper Englishman. League of British Patriots.

ZENA.   Red, white and blue!

MOSCROP *indicates subtly for the* BEVINS *to begin filling in the grave. They clump over.*

ST LEGER.   Au Revoir, Auf Wiedersehen, Arivederci, Princess Rakoskaya, Knightsbridge.

ZENA.   Who's she when she's at home?

ST LEGER.   Never heard of her. One of his bints. *(As* ST LEGER *reads on, camera closes on* MOSCROP's *face. The sound of earth falling in the grave slowly obscures the conversation.)* Goodbye, Sir Den, Staff and Pupils, St Enochs Primary School.

ZENA.   Ahhhh. . . .

ST LEGER.   Woman's Guild . . . British Legion. . . .

ZENA.   Little pillow, ain't that nice?

ST LEGER.   Farmers' Union. . . .

The screen goes black. Credits.